T0146677

ALL POLLEN, NO PETAL

BEHIND THE FLOWER FARMING DREAM

RALPH THURSTON

authorHOUSE®

AuthorHouse™
1663 Liberty Drive
Bloomington, IN 47403
www.authorhouse.com
Phone: 1 (800) 839-8640

Published by AuthorHouse   05/10/2018

ISBN: 978-1-5462-4188-1 (sc)
ISBN: 978-1-5462-4189-8 (e)

Print information available on the last page.

Any people depicted in stock imagery provided by Getty Images are models, and such images are being used for illustrative purposes only. Certain stock imagery © Getty Images.

This book is printed on acid-free paper.

CONTENTS

INTRODUCTION

L OCALS USE THE phrase "all hat, no cattle" to describe pretend cowboys, those packaged like ranchers but lacking their substance, their ethic and talent. There's a difference between "the dream" and the work, between appearance and essence, wrapping and contents, and in many respects cut flower farming is much the same, the dream being "all petal, no pollen", all surface, no substance. *All Pollen, No Petal* exposes the substance.

Just as cowboying entails dust and wind and sweat and dung, flower farming is about less than picturesque things like dirt and weeds, fungus and insects and compost heaps. That's why you won't see pictures in this book. That and the fact that once you start choosing flower photos it's impossible to stop—pretty soon it just all becomes pictures and the words fall away.

But unlike ranching, flower farming IS all about appearance, which may explain the renaissance going on now. The Internet brings pretty images right to the pajama wearing surfer's home, allowing a bit of dreaming in perfect comfort. Beauty is alluring, and we seem genetically programmed to reach for the glitter, for the shiny, for color. Hence, a proliferation of mostly small and local farms after a three decade American flower industry hiatus. Thousands of new growers, mostly young but some older, some already experienced but most entering only with ambition, a little gardening experience, and a love of beauty and flowers, have flocked to the occupation and more keep coming.

Having started growing flowers as the industry faded decades ago, it's a bit alarming to me. I didn't have Google, I didn't even have the Internet, and county agricultural agents responded to my questions ready to dial 911 for help, thinking I was a bit "tetched in the head". I'm envious of the networking available now but ambivalent toward the information (and misinformation) barrage, and maybe a bit sorry I wasn't part of a movement—most of us who started farming had only the ASCFG and an occasional conference to keep us tethered to the farming world, and we have no idea what it would be like to be part of the vibrant group extant now, on our way up instead of on our way out.

Envious as I am, I remember the long and difficult process it took to get from total greenhorn to successful grower, from stars-in-the-eyes to thorns-in-the-thumb, and I look at the new crop of growers just as I look at my own crops: hopeful they succeed, knowing there's a good chance many will fail. I've lived long enough to witness the housing boom and crash of 2008, the dot-com boom in the 90's, am acquainted with the history of the Tulip Frenzy in Holland, the Gold Rushes in California and Alaska, the land grab that quickly turned the Great Plains into the Dust Bowl, so I know there's a downside to rapid expansion. My fingers are crossed for the young grower influx.

Though hoping the flower farming boom has a long time to play out before it goes bust, I know all sorts flock to promise—to seek, to aid the seeker, to prey on the seeker—and in the swarm of activity and excitement of a trend it's hard to sort through what's pie-in-the-sky and what's actually possible. I wrote *All Pollen, No Petal* to address the space between those two things.

All Pollen is intended for those already embarked upon the chaotic journey of flower farming and those just considering it, and it aims to dissuade the unsuspecting from jumping into the field without knowing what they're up against—so the dream of farming flowers and running a business of their own doesn't become a nightmare. I love flower farming but it's not for everyone—like cigarettes, it requires a disclaimer on its package.

My wife (Jeriann Sabin) and I started Bindweed Farm sometime around 1991—the exact date of its beginning, like most conceptions, being of somewhat dubious nature. It morphed from leafcutter bee habitat to dried flower production to farmer's market fresh cut sales to a local florist route and deliveries to wholesalers. Finally, we took up our own bucket routes to resort areas with more flower-savvy and flower-hungry clients than we'd been accustomed to or even known about. We reached four acres of production in size, growing woody shrubs, perennials, annuals and bulbs before we sold the farm and retired this spring, outlasting a half dozen wholesalers and scores of designers who retired or were forced from business as the globalization shuffle took place. Surviving, too, hundreds of our own mistakes, weather events, insect infestations and crop failures that hardened us off without destroying us.

We eventually reached nearly two hundred thousand dollars in annual sales, making it happen on four acres and a couple two thousand square foot greenhouses in a 120 day growing season, working by ourselves and aided by a couple part-time summer helpers. We know smarter growers, sharper businesspeople, much more clever marketers, and others who, given our fortunate niche, would have far outperformed us, but we're still amazed, and it's that amazement that kept us enthralled even as our energies waned—we think we understand why businessmen become obsessed with work: it's not so much about success or ego or greed as the rush that comes when an idea and effort unfolds. When something, essentially, blooms.

You may have read our book *Deadhead: The Bindweed Way of Growing Flowers,* which we wrote as a team to give new and old, warm climate and cold area flower farmers alike our vision of how to go about the peculiar business of cut flowers and negotiate its nooks and crannies. *All Pollen, No Petal* is *Deadhead's* dark-side sequel that comes with three parts, the first looking at oft-neglected, even unseemly aspects of flower farming and the tasks every farmer faces: weeding, cutting, and irrigating. The second section has more specific advice for growers, and the third part, The Deadhead Employee/Employer Handbook concentrates on the difficult relationship between owners and workers—a problem not, by any means, singular to farming, but one exacerbated by its conflicting characteristics in being of seasonal nature but having high-skill, high-knowledge requirements.

We hope *All Pollen* helps you, as a reader, either toward a dream you should chase or, conversely, away from a nightmare you should avoid.

PART ONE

ALL POLLEN

MOTHER NATURE

I DON'T KNOW HOW nature got misnamed as a mother, unless someone left off a second, more vulgar word that sometimes attaches to the term, because more than anything nature resembles not a mother but a young child—a child with a crayon let loose in a well-kept, well-swept home with nice white walls just waiting to be writ upon. Now would Mom do the things that child would do? Really—hailstorms, insects, weeds: are these the actions associated with motherhood?

Maybe, if your mom was an abusive alcoholic.

No, nature's a child, and she wants to scribble on anything, then scribble over the scribbling. And she colors outside the lines! To her there are no lines, in fact, no border that can't be crossed, no fence that can't be bridged. Such manmade devices are but challenges, really, and she's happy to accept and transcend them.

If you are raising a small child, you might be equipped to deal with nature.

You know that a child stays within boundaries only if you consistently maintain them and that you minimize chaos by dealing with transgressions earlier rather than later. Farming's much the same, it's best to deal with problems early and to maintain the lines you draw. Good luck with that…

It's not an easy task, because you have a property line that the wind doesn't respect as it lifts the neighbor's weed seed in for you to deal with for years to come. Animals ignore its legal aspect, going through and over and around the fences, burrowing beneath them. If you irrigate, drawing a line in time, the clouds ignore you, dumping another couple inches of rain on your transplants, coloring over the schedule you've made for future tasks. It's a schedule that seems logical and unobtrusive but which Little Nancy Nature treats as a bit of playground fun, a jungle gym to climb through and inadvertently wreck.

Even the lines you draw for other humans need vigilant maintenance, orders and requests and deliveries getting tossed about by clients much as tormenters play keep-away with a helpless child. Your employee starts coming five minutes late, wants a day off in high season. A designer changes her order at the last minute. Your plug producer fails to ship your entire order. You might start feeling picked-on, get a bit of a victim complex. But you need to remember there are no lines in nature. Whatever lines you see, you made, so if you're a victim, you're a victim of your own perpetration.

You can call a shoreline a shoreline, but it constantly moves over time. What's water now is sand later, what's sand now is water later. And then sand again. You can call a family a family and it looks quite obvious until you look closer—does it include your stepbrother, your in-laws, and if it includes them, does it include their in-laws and their stepbrothers? Where do you stop? That "ecosystem" on your farm? The line you drew in your mind where you arranged a diverse array of species and treated them with eco-friendliness and Integrated Pest Management so that the harmony of nature's beings interacted in a symbiotic manner? Well, the neighbor's aphids and lygus bugs don't respect that line when they take flight after his hay's cut, and the gopher doesn't see it, nor does the vole or the beaver or the raccoon. And the deer and elk and moose have different plans than you, too.

And what about the insolence regarding your irrigation schedule, where you separated time into such tidy parcels—four hours on the sunflowers, three in the greenhouses, a couple on the new transplants? It gets only disrespect from the next rainstorm or hot, dry wind. The tears in the drip tape that the voles made give no respect, the valve that breaks when you turn it ruins the little water-dance you created, the filters plug, someone hoed a line, you forgot to open a line, the breaker fails and knocks the pump off—it's as if no one and nothing pays heed to the lines you've drawn.

And those nice grass pathways, such elegant lines when constructed and intended to make your work easier and keep the flowers clean, well, the grass creeps into the flower beds they're supposed to separate, and threaten to become not a thing-between but the entire thing itself.

Oh, don't forget the lines you bring on a higher, intellectual level, your ideas about the world that a flower-farming friend described as "just cartoons" inside her head. Maps upon the world, recipes for action, things you thought you knew that you learned from googling and reading books, that you heard at conferences. Well, they won't necessarily structure your experience in the field. You're lucky if they coincide in any way with what happens on a daily basis. You find that companion planting proves ineffective, the homemade insect repellent someone swore by is a waste of time, resources and effort. Limiting your carbon footprint and aligning your actions with nature, upon further scrutiny, seems more to limit your income and align you with poverty.

Concepts, ideas, preconceptions, techniques, methods, they're all lines that get in the way of direct perception. For those expounding them they reign in the chaos, perhaps after a lifetime perfecting their ideas, but when you receive those ideas remember that the givers are a long way down the path you're starting on, that you're taking art lessons from Picasso, basketball lessons from Stephen Curry, golf lessons from Tiger Woods, music lessons from Yo-Yo Ma—the books you read and the people you listen to may have something to offer, but you're a long way from having their talents and experience and likely won't get the same results that they do. Not at first, anyway.

If you try to assimilate new products and methods into your endeavor, thinking of them as magical and easy, you'll likely create a chaos exceeding that of our young child with a crayon. You're adding obstacles rather than easing yourself through nature's trickery. When Nancy Nature wields her box of crayons, at least you can erase her graffiti, but the crayon marks of humans are sometimes indelible.

Xeriscape, permaculture, aquaponics, organic, sustainable, no-till, French double-dig—if you've lived long enough, you've seen scores of "the latest" things appear and disappear and reappear. Treat them openly but with skepticism, treat them like fads or the stock market, where there are always two things going on—the "real" and the speculative, with the speculative sometimes affecting the real. Take a deep look at the ideas and assess them—do they make sense, are they researched, or are they anecdotal in nature and seem too good to be true? Take a deep look at yourself and assess what you see: just how gullible are you, do you just WANT to believe them, do they hit you in a spot that makes you feel good? No idea, no thing is entirely good, so if you feel a thing is magic, distrust yourself. Enjoy the moment, but distrust yourself. Farming's going to take work, things aren't going to take care of themselves once you set your operation into motion—no matter how many tools and methods (lines, really) you bring to your land.

As you move from the computer and book to the field, your vision will adjust, just as a set of transition glasses does as you move from shade to light. If your sight doesn't adjust, you'll quickly fail. Though nature has no lines she has rules she insistently enforces. She's not going to bow to your belief systems, your methods, your lines. She's factual, physical, in a take-it-or-leave-it-I-don't care-which sort of way. Neither malignant nor beneficent, she gives equal opportunity to aphids and ladybugs alike—she may like aphids a bit more, in fact, since ladybugs need aphids to live but aphids don't need ladybugs, making the aphids more fundamentally valuable.

By all means, you can still bring your lines, your tools, your baggage, with you, but drag the whole slew of them rather than pushing them out in front of you. If you can, just consider them as your carry-on, ready to use in the stowaway compartment should you need them, but hopefully left untouched for the entirety of your journey.

Once you learn nature has no lines don't breathe too easy, there's more bad news. There is yet another set of lines to negotiate. All those lines you set aside—well, everyone else has a set, too, and even if you eliminate yours you still have to figure out theirs. There'll be innumerable ones you've already assimilated and as many that you haven't. Property lines, business regulations, government requirements, explicitly, but implicit ones like fashion, style, quality standards, quantity standards, monetary agreements, interpersonal interactions—it's a fairly interminable list. And as whimsical as nature's rules might seem they're at least predictable, while man's lines turn on a whim that may transform into instant trauma.

You're going to wonder why what's good enough for you isn't good enough for your client. You'll wonder how others don't find the same things beautiful, or worth as much. Their standards of quality may be higher—what's a few aphids, you think, whereas they're aghast. If you're accustomed to thinking of things as right and wrong you may be in trouble, and if you think you're always right you're really in trouble. The categories are simply this: profitable and not profitable. If you insist on your standards as right and the rest of the world's as wrong, you'll probably fit in the last, unprofitable, category.

Learn your mental and emotional lines. You bring them to your decision making process whether you know it or not. The world, both natural and social, gives you a wide-open, fairly unlimited palette to work upon, and then you slice it up into manageable bits, often unknowingly. It's the normal state for an effective organism, because the world possesses way too many details for any single being to assimilate. But—and it's a big but—once your brain downsizes the infinite world to its local, workable context, your prejudices shrink it further, so much so that they often lead to failure. These prejudices, whether learned unconsciously or purposefully adopted, likely hinder your actions. If you're aware of them and wish to keep them, you can knowingly continue your actions knowing YOU and not the world thwarted your efforts, but if you're not aware you may resent the world and blame others for what you've done.

For every refined method you choose in your farming enterprise, you shrink your palette. You choose not to use chemicals—the world shrinks. You choose sustainability—it shrinks a bit further. You want to be organic—ditto. No till—moreso. Permaculture—yet a smaller world in which to operate. You can actually argue yourself right out of existence, and that's not good. Because just the fact that you care enough to try to make things better makes you invaluable to the rest of us—the world needs you, even if you aren't perfect, because at least you haven't given up trying to be so.

As your possibilities shrink, the difficulty of farming rises. The perfect way, being perfect, has a single chance among infinite possibilities—work out the equation, it's just math, and you're aiming for the unlikely in terms of success. If you decide not to be perfect, your world widens, probabilities rise, success becomes more likely, though your idealism will go the way of collateral damage.

If you just want to make money, the path there is a singular one. For every additional constriction you place upon that desire, you shrink the width of your paths, shrink the possibilities of reaching your goal and lengthen the time it takes to get there. Your effort may be noble, but don't be so foolish as not to know that you, only you, chose to hinder your own progress.

MONEY VS. LIFESTYLE

A LOT OF FLOWER growers get into the business because they like flowers, or like to grow flowers, or like the idea of growing flowers, and most of them just kind of hope that the money and business end of that is a happy byproduct—a "build it and they will come" feeling.

There's a great deal of non-monetary income from getting your hands dirty, planting, harvesting, seeing color and shape arise and abundance proliferate, and there's a great deal of bodily good to reap from toil, fresh air to glean from the job, sunlight to bask in—in a desk job you might not earn any of these things. Still, as the saying goes, "scenery don't butter no parsnips" and you can't trade flowers for a car or electricity, much less for gall bladder surgery or taxes. Only money takes care of those things.

So it's down to math, down to money. What a

bummer, but it doesn't have to mean JUST money, you can count your rewards in other ways—the exercise, the joy, the good will of farming. Nonetheless, you do have to in some way quantify non-monetary expenditures and income to understand their value. It turns your decision making from the difficult either/or of money or lifestyle, into a more/less, which enables you to have your cake and eat at least some of it.

But you have to realize there's no objective value to what you do, outside of the product you provide. There's no blue book detailing the worth of your joy. Don't expect others to value it the same. They're not going to pay you more for your flowers just because you enjoy cutting them. And though they might like local flowers better than those trucked in from another continent, though they might prefer organic flowers to those chemically grown, there's a limit to their goodwill. Money talks, despite our denials. If you disagree, do a thought experiment on anything— an apple, for instance. Will you pay a dollar for an organic apple when a conventionally grown one costs fifty cents? Two dollars? Ten? Twenty? Up the number, sooner or later you have a limit. The point here is to not kid yourself into thinking it's not about money. We wish it wasn't about money, we can make it so it's not about money entirely, but it's still, at root, about supporting ourselves and our lifestyles—via the use of money. We just have to decide how extensively money is going to infiltrate the more pleasurable aspects of our endeavor.

So, we're comparing apples and oranges here, money and lifestyle, but frankly, that's life, isn't it? We compare incommensurable things all the time, weigh the benefits of one thing against others despite their differences—getting married to the ugly and mean but rich laird or to the kind, handsome peasant, for instance. The apple here is a livelihood, a business, a way to make money to buy all the other things you need—warmth, shelter, food, skinny vanilla lattes, and such. All the apples are easy to measure in monetary terms—you pay such an amount for a plant, it costs this amount to raise, you sell it for X and pocket Y. Simple. Less simple is evaluating the oranges, the costs and benefits of the other aspects of your enterprise: how much is my lifestyle benefitting me, how much is it costing me? I get to spend all my time at home, a benefit, perhaps, but I'm always at work, a cost. Or vice versa, or a combination of both. I'm pleased that I'm farming sustainably, less pleased that my high tech farming neighbor's making more money and seems to have an easier time of things. I get to be my own boss, but I have to be responsible for everything I do. No vacations, no days off—but I can take a break when I need it, have a snack when I'm hungry.

There'll always be a tension between your monetary wishes and your lifestyle desires, so you need to get clear early in your farm's history on just what's more important and just how much more important. Once you understand fully your aims, when the choices that pit the two things against each other arise (and arise they do, constantly) you won't waste emotional energy and decision time weighing what action you should take. Aphids are going to take over—do I spray chemical and take care of them or let my crop go to nature? Do I work with this Bridezilla, make tons of money and suffer her wrath, or do I pass on the job and avoid that stress? These sorts of questions arise in any business or endeavor, and the better you understand your direction and commitment to that direction the less time and energy you'll spend with internal conflicts. And, by taking charge of your decisions you put less negativity (in the forms of blame and resentment) out into the universe—no one made you do it, the world didn't force your decision.

BEAUTY—NOT

B EAUTY. IF YOU'RE a flower farmer it's your business.

So you think.

Well, it's not. Flower farming is—producing things that others think are beautiful.

So, just as flowers evolved to draw bees in to pollinate them so they could make seed, beauty has evolved to draw you in to start flower farming. It worked. It got you started. Now the most fun part's over and the business of production gets underway. You can still have fun, it's just that it'll be adult fun, not childish imaginings. You're a farmer, not a beautician. Unless your farming endeavor includes designing flowers as part of the business, in which case temper the reading of what's to come.

You don't have to give up beauty, but you do have to get over it being the primary drive of your business. When we bought our first foot of drip tape, the local nursery owner (who pointedly asked us "why not grow locally, who said it can't be done?" thereby sending us on our way), who also owned a flower shop, remarked how difficult it was to get efficient help. "They all think they're artists," he complained, rolling his eyes, referring to their need to aim for that perfect arrangement, simultaneously taking up time for which he was paying. He didn't know that Jeriann was an artist.

You have to concede that you're in business to make money and give up a bit of artistry, concede to efficiency in time and resource, submit to thinking about profit and loss, start thinking about wasted time and effort and all those things that the real world's about. You don't have to completely give up beauty or the wish to have your own business and do work you love, but you do have to find where the interface, for you, will be where you're willing to give up either earnings or ideals.

If you want to starve, you'll give up earnings. If you want to become crass and cynical, you'll give up ideals. If you can't find a balance between the two that satisfies you, you best not start your enterprise. If you think you can give up earnings because you have so few needs, you better look closely at your life: do you like plumbing? Phones? Tattoos? Movies? Warmth? Shelter? Good food? Those things don't come out of nowhere, you've just put the thought of them away into a default compartment you rarely revisit.

You kind of know *what* you want, probably a life of pleasurable work that provides a comfortable living, but you need to determine *how much* a comfortable living requires and *how much* unpleasant work you can tolerate. If you don't do this minimal thought exercise, if you just compartmentalize this into the "I'll think about it later" box, you're aiming for either mental dissonance or exporting the same to those around you, because the world is full of facts that refuse to respond to your thoughts about them and your insistence that they be otherwise.

If you think ten thousand dollars in profit will get you by, realize you need to sell twice that in product to take care of expenses. If it's twenty, you need to sell forty. This varies, of course, and most businesses would be thrilled to have a ten percent profit margin, so situate yourself in reality and know that infrastructure costs—which might be nearly nothing when you start since you likely have a shoestring operation—increase in the second phase when you realize you need more sales and might actually make the enterprise work. That's when you start buying things to make the business possible: land, tractors, equipment, nursery stock. And you may need labor help, so your profit percentage shrinks a bit more—as does the joy of working alone. The bigger you get, the wider net you cast, the more infrastructure you need and the less profit you pull in—it's why farmers often get called rich in possessions but "cash-poor", because they have land, tools, machinery, having poured their profits back into the business, but may have very little in savings or retirement funds.

Thinking about money might be unpleasant but at least the subject's measurable. The unpleasantness of work can't be measured or foreseen. If you've only raised a small garden, picked a few flowers, put some bouquets together, basked in the smells and textures of the plant world, you won't be ready for the big change that comes when you increase your square footage of production space or when you multiply the hours spent taking care of the plants upon it. You may find an hour weeding your garden pleasant, doing it six hours a day may not be. You might enjoy watering your plants for an hour or two in your yard, but find irrigation on half an acre troublesome, worrisome, distasteful and seemingly impossible.

And then there are the sudden pressures of business itself: pleasing clients, meeting their demands, having enough product, having quality product, fighting pests and diseases, suffering the weather and buffering against it when you can. Can you deal with this? Beauty and pleasantries often fall by the wayside when the list of reality's demands lengthens.

You don't have to give up on beauty, you don't have to place it in opposition to the less pleasurable actions of farming. You just have to put it on hold—it's like an emergency room (or a MASH unit, if you're old enough to remember that TV show), where triage determines who or what needs help most urgently: harvest first, bugs and disease second, weeds third, and beauty last, because beauty survives, it needs no help. You'll still understand the persistence of beauty every time a new species comes to bloom, every time you harvest a bucket of flowers and see its color pop in the morning sunlight, and every time you consider how your hands, your efforts brought this all to fruition. Nature's a remarkable thing, flowers perhaps the most remarkable of all her offerings, and those who tend them and interact with her are the real caretakers of existence.

Beauty is about perfection, aesthetic perfection, relationships between elements, shape, form, texture, and color. Likely, the thought alone of beauty titillates you—that's what got you started on your venture. Perfect ideas, like beauty, do that to us, they enrich us, lift us, enthrall us. Once you've experienced them you can't imagine life without them.

But they throw us off track.

So join the crowd. Every boy who ever picked up a football wants to be an NFL player, everyone who enjoyed reading thinks himself a writer, every kid who ever had refrigerator art thinks she's an artist. We're fools, for the most part, Homo Jesteris, rather than Homo Habilis the tool user or Homo Sapiens, it's what separates us from other species. We're fools because in any field, any endeavor, there is only one perfect, which may not actually exist, and a myriad foolish imperfects both possible and real. It's a pyramid—its pinnacle is what we aim for, its base is where we start, and the climb to the top becomes more difficult as we move from wholly imperfect to slightly imperfect and finally to perfect (if the top hasn't been eroded away). We can be Buddhalike or Christlike, but we can't be Buddha or Christ.

In any field, and you can include flower farming, it takes considerable skill and expertise to get to A- (pretty good) but it's at least within reach. But to get to A+, that little bit better than A-, takes an extraordinary amount of effort. Be it design work, musicianship, or athleticism, only a few get decent returns from the leap from pretty good to nigh-perfect. As a business person, you want to think about least output for greatest rewards, so if you're in it for the money you best aim for a little less than perfect. Only those few at the top earn the big bucks just for being who they are, for having the reputation they've gained, and for having the talent to get there—talent you might very well have but which you aren't willing to exploit because of choices you make that restrain it.

Settling for less won't be easy. Since beauty is really the aim of the game it's hard to drop all the things you've learned about aesthetic pleasure and pick up the tools of the world to actually make a living. If you design, you can't be circling your effort again and again looking for imperfections, searching for that perfect thing that completes it, or you'll never get it out to the wedding venue. You'll be there forever, because an artist's work is never done. The world's in motion, and the artist takes a project at one moment and completes it, but upon completing it starts seeing an entirely different project which again needs completing. Instance one becomes instance two becomes instance three, and while the mind can imagine completion, nature and reality can't. Artists should lease, not sell, their work, so they can come into your house and "fix" the flaws they inevitably see in what they've done.

Isn't the effort to be perfect the problem? It's the extra work and effort that takes you from real good to perfect that strains any organism, any system. The welfare system becomes inefficient as we try to prevent cheating by adding extra layers to guard against waste, but if we built in an acceptance of a small amount of cheating to occur, our money could go to the intended recipients rather than to government bureaucrats. A football game deteriorates when we have instant replay on every call, trying to make sure referees are perfect. Bureaucratic forms and owner's manuals become difficult because the makers try to cover every possibility. If we tolerate a few imperfections, a little cheating, a little failure, results come easier and inputs and efforts shrink.

It's been said that ugly can be beautiful but cute never can. When we say "don't get cute", we're admonishing someone who's trying just a little too hard to be perfect, taking too much time doing so, wasting energy, using too much money, expanding a simple process into a complex one. Perfect can be too perfect, that's why Zen pottery requires a flaw to be in every piece—a crack, a discoloration—and why magazine models need a beauty mark that some think disfiguring. Think of your farm as a place that tolerates that slight imperfection, think of your movement away from mere indulgence of beauty as a movement toward a more adult version of shaping your life and your portion of the world toward the beautiful—creating it, rather than absorbing it, trusting it on its own rather than controlling it to conform to your expectations.

HIT 'EM WHERE THEY AIN'T

W HEN ASKED HOW he was such an effective hitter, Wee Willie Keeler famously replied "I hit 'em where they ain't". Take his words as sagely advice—an early twentieth century example of Taoist wisdom. What does it mean? If everyone else is doing it, don't do it, if everyone's selling it, don't sell it, if everyone's growing it, don't grow it. Don't get in line, don't copy, don't compete against everyone, instead find an open space that yields to your efforts.

Don't jump on trends unless you have a talent for recognizing them. When you were in junior high school, did you know when a fashion was on the upswing or spiraling downward? If you were the "it" girl, you probably have a handle on what's hot, if you were a lagger, slow to assimilate the "in" thing, don't jump into something wholeheartedly or you'll fail. If you're not a trendsetter yourself, lurk in the penumbra of one, pay attention not to those with similar tastes (since yours don't agree with what's hot) but those ahead of you. And pay attention to those behind, too—we had a client hang on to dried flowers for a decade after they became passé, and when she recently dispatched her inventory we nodded and said "drieds are coming back in." Indeed they were, after twenty years being out of vogue.

Most any fad or trend is a bit of a pyramid scheme, with early entrants cashing in and latecomers in the feeding frenzy funneling money to those getting there first. Read up on the tulip craze several centuries ago in Holland and you'll catch a glimpse of the bubble mentality, the boom-and-bust tendencies that make humans more like lemmings than hyperconscious beings. Sometimes it's the fear of being left behind that actually puts you behind—if your instinct tells you to sit this one out, pay attention. Catch the next horse on the merry-go-round of fashion, but catch it early.

Most new growers feel confident of their style and fashion sense. They wouldn't be involved in flowers if they didn't understand the importance of appearance. You may be confident of what colors, designs and species currently hold sway because you already are riding the currents as a designer or even as just a follower of Pinterest, but don't extrapolate that "feel" for flowers and color into other trends, like business—your confidence in a field you've worked in for years doesn't necessarily transpose into all other genres.

One such trend is ecommerce. Almost every business needs a web presence these days, just like they needed river or ocean frontage when boats were the primary commercial vehicles, highway frontage when cars came into being, railroad sidings when that route was primary for economic sustenance. Clients don't look in the phone book any more and many don't even look for brick and mortar stores, instead they look on the web. You need to be there.

So get yourself a website, have an Instagram account, maybe even tweet, but align your web presence with the type of business you run because, as is the case when any new platform for distribution arises, a cottage industry of charlatans are out there trying to sell you more than you need. If you recently registered a web site you likely got an immediate spam folder full of offers to design your site, telling you what its shortcomings are and how they can help, and even locally you might be approached by entrepreneurs cashing in on the social media trend. Some are intentionally cheating you, some are overconfident and some believe what they sell, but the outcome of either good or bad intentions results in the same for you—a waste of time and money. If you really need a massive web presence because you want to widen your base to include the whole nation or the world, by all means sort through the chaff and find an honorable and able web designer to blast your business upon the universe, but if you just want to sell locally, design locally, do events locally, you can likely take care of your social media existence by yourself. You don't need a high-priced photographer, just a good one (maybe even yourself), you don't need a highly paid consultant and may not need a consultant at all, and you shouldn't believe every person who talks about things actually knows about them—don't overstate your ignorance, it may just be healthy skepticism, and don't overestimate their knowledge, it may just be jargon and hype.

If you have a regular client list with no desire for more (or no hope for more since your base area is small, like ours), all you need is a basic site with current availability list, pictures of your offerings, your phone number, possibly a way to order. Many new growers think they need to constantly blog or consistently post Instagram pictures so they can boast of thousands of followers, but the number of followers doesn't necessarily correlate with business. We posted a tulip planting video that received twelve thousand views but got no verifiable business from the post—we weren't looking for extra business, it's true, but it is evidence that just being looked at means absolutely nothing. If you don't have anything to sell, you don't need three hundred thousand followers, and even if you do have that big of a following it doesn't legitimize your business.

It takes a particular personality to be a good promoter, and many farmers just want to farm and dislike that end of the business. You have to like it to do it well, just like you likely farm better if you like to farm. Size your visible presence according to what you want or need and your ability to provide it. If you fear being behind because you see web "friends" with a hundred thousand followers, remember a couple things: 1) there's a snowball effect on the web that's driven by mathematical algorithms and those algorithms can be manipulated by computer specialists; 2) Like the stock market, the more believers or followers or investors you get the more join in, thinking to get a piece of the action—more begets more, but that doesn't mean anything of substance stands behind the appearance; 3) A business can be all show and no go, because rarely do we get to see the bottom line of those who appear successful; who knows if they actually make money from what they do, you may actually be more monetarily successful than them without even knowing—they're just more visible. Recently, a blogger with a big presence of hundreds of thousands of followers grew tired of the whole run-and-chase aspect of her business and exposed how she had gained her fame: she'd bought it by using programmers who guaranteed to make her go viral.

If you want to be big, by all means go big with your social media, but don't be fooled into thinking you need a massive horde of followers. You may just need relationships, and that's done by personal interactions repeated over time, and establishing connections through the media that your customers use. Telephone replaced face-to-face interaction, fax replaced telephone, email replaced fax, and text replaced email, and each step along the way businesspeople needed to change with the times, but along the way of change came a cast of characters cashing in on the fear of being behind, overselling the change to unsuspecting people. Don't be one of the unsuspecting.

NEUROTIC OR PSYCHOTIC?

———✦~◈~✦———

E VERY SPRING A local truck farmer swings by to shoot the breeze, the conversation inevitably turning to how he might up his game, expand his market, make his operation profitable enough to quit his job, leave its steady paycheck and benefits. I run a few ideas by him—grow specialty crops, become the leader in food knowledge so his customers trust him when he grows something new, eat differently and cook differently and pass his knowledge on, learn what his clients want, use a less costly, more efficient method—and he counters every suggestion: he can't (or won't), he's not set up for that, he doesn't know if such a client base exists, *that wouldn't work*, his family wouldn't like to eat that way, he doesn't know how to grow it. It turns out what he wants is not to change but for the world to change, but if you want things to change, you need to change something *you* do. Though you might have heard otherwise, it's easier for Moses to go to the mountain than to bring the mountain to Moses.

There's an easy way to look at this particular quirk of action, and let's misinterpret Freud a bit in order to do so: a neurotic is someone who wants the entire world to come to him and a psychotic is someone who wants to inundate the world with himself. Now, you can approach the world neurotically—build it and they will come, is one variation of that approach, whining-without-doing is more common—and you can approach it psychotically. Traditional farmers get blamed for the latter, their methods of heavy tillage, genetic manipulation and chemical use often demonized by others.

But organic farmers can behave psychotically, too, imposing their will upon the world with methods of only anecdotal merit, methods that only highly skilled professionals can pull off. They consider themselves to be working *with* nature though they're imposing their preconceptions *upon* it. Organic farmers sometimes practice neurotically, too, prancing through the soil, dropping seeds in the soil for a benevolent nature to turn to marketable blooms—that's how we started (and it didn't end pretty). Occasionally even ridiculous methods work, nature mending mistakes or markets smiling simply because we're the first guest to arrive.

Any method, psychotic or neurotic, plays best on a blank slate—an empty piece of paper provides no obstacle. Idaho's late billionaire potato mogul J.R. Simplot described the perfect crop rotation as a "thousand years of sagebrush, one year of potatoes", because he saw early farmers encountering untapped rich, volcanic soil that provided good crops to even the lowly skilled. And in another stroke of fortune, in his early career the potato market approached the nearly infinite, hundreds of thousands of WWII troops needing food overseas and dehydrated spuds being perfect to ship. Two blank slates—untouched farmground, untouched markets—brought him and the Idaho potato industry nearly instant fortune. Few such virgin territories exist anymore.

You can impose your will, make rash decisions, or you can let the world impose its will upon you and hope nature's will conforms to your desires. There's a spectrum of actions reaching from doing nothing (permaculture tends toward that side) to doing everything possible ("The Martian" agronomy, where all inputs are controlled) and you'll be wavering across the spectrum as you decide how to confront problems that arise.

Building a new house is easier than redoing an old one. Starting a new government in a new land, as the US did, is easier than starting a democracy in a millennia old Middle Eastern culture where old relationships, grudges, and memories entwine. And farming on virgin soil in an ecosystem lacking crop enemies is easier than wedging your way into a chaotic, long-tilled acreage where pests proliferate for every species. The first settlers here needed only to understand a little about farming. Many probably thought they understood it, but came from different climates, different soil types and different native species and were shocked with what they encountered. Those fixing upon what they knew, who tried to impose old world understanding on the new world, failed, but those who put their old lines and baggage behind them (but utilized them where appropriate) and paid attention to the new relationships between species, climate and soil succeeded.

You, as a new settler in an old world, have to understand not only nature's habits but those of every person who used the land before you. In a perfect world, you'd have a list of their habits, of the new species introduced (both intentionally and unintentionally), a tally of what was done over the years—was the ground leveled, was the soil amended or depleted, were animals raised in certain areas, what invasive species came—but unless you've lived close by for years (and paid attention as you did) you won't know the ground you'll be working.

If you're looking for farmground, don't look in the winter. Unless you're sure of the farm's history, you can't see what you're buying. It's best to eye the property the year before and pay close attention. If it's bare in the spring, wait for rain—the water will expose gravel and rock and you can decide if it's worth your work. Does winter runoff pond, thus ruining the soil there? And was the winter's precipitation close enough to normal to determine its spring effects? Take a shovelful of soil and test your PH and nutrient content to see what you can grow and what amendments you might need to fix it. Later in the year walk carefully through the tract, look for perennial weeds like bindweed (morning glory), horsetail, quackgrass, thistle. If these or other noxious weeds exist, your task is going to be more difficult. Dealing with annual weeds is usually doable, given enough diligence and patience, but the most noxious perennials may take decades to eradicate—even with chemical.

Most new farmers meet their most difficult challenges in the beginning of their careers, and most don't meet those challenges and so end their careers early. Because they try to impose their ideas on already vibrant ecosystems, jumping into a tango as if it might be a square dance, nature rebuffs them. You can avoid this by starting interaction with your farm ready for problems, rather than naively thinking you're sharp-witted enough to do what others haven't been able to do. Even if you know a lot in general you may not know what you need to about this specific piece of ground.

If you don't mind being a psychotic farmer, you can avoid the painful courtship by applying fumigants to the soil that kill all seeds, good or bad, and all living things, good or bad. This means you won't have to deal with weeds for a few years, forever if you become an attentive steward, and you won't have to deal with pests for awhile. It also means, of course, that you've destroyed, for a time, the vibrancy of the soil's organisms, so you'll need to be cognizant of restoring the soil to health. If you don't want to take the drastic route, you need to ease your way into working the new farm. Don't waste money on weed fabric until you know the severity of your weed problem, because rhizomatous weeds still find their way into holes cut into the fabric. Once you have perennial rhizomes under control, apply fabric as you desire.

Plant fast germinators, quick growers, large seeds that don't require as much contact with soil, since new ground, when first tilled, rarely provides the proper texture that small seeds need—there are too many air pockets, for instance, in land just out of pasture or hay.

Since it takes years to really know a piece of ground and you want to start making money soon, you need to learn quickly. But act deftly. Wisely. Don't impose yourself upon the land, don't let nature impose itself upon you, and don't ask the world to comply to your wishes— you can ask, but don't expect the answer you want to hear.

SPILLS

MOST FARMERS IN this part of Idaho grow the same crop—sugar beets, potatoes, barley and wheat, maybe alfalfa and pasture if they work with cattle—so most have similar needs and habits. Irrigation-wise, many draw cheap water from a canal system and they like their pumps to turn off a couple hours before dawn so they can move the drained lines as the sun comes up, and then in mid-afternoon they turn them off again to move the lines before dusk. Add to this their religious habits—laborless (and thus irrigation-less) Sundays—and another variable enters into a canal manager's equation. It's a century old joke that if you want all the water you need, just wait until Sunday and you can steal all the water you want. Technology's demands and farmers' habits create an up and down demand difficult to manage when water flow depends on the unchanging laws of gravity.

Any producer of goods deals with such fluctuations—the

flower grower's compost pile tells you how well he deals with his. The more dependable a grower is to his clients the more risk they ask him to take—they move the monkey from their desk and put it on his, and, unless he's a great monkey trainer, he chases it out to the compost heap.

That monkey has a lot of quirky characteristics: a requested species needs to come to bloom at the right time—bloom time can vary, wedding dates cannot; there has to be enough product to supply an event—the order doesn't change, but yields do. The list of uncertainties may be longer than the list of certainties, so the grower, wanting to be sure to provide *enough* product must grow *too much*. And since he grows too much (if he grows too little he loses his reputation) he needs a place to dispose of the disorder accepted from his clients—that place may be secondary clients, emergency outlets, charities, the compost, or simply unharvested in the field.

To be fair, the clients' needs vary, too, *their* clients exporting *their* risk to the designer. Maybe a spur of the moment wedding gets sandwiched into the normal business flow, or a political group sets up a fundraiser and needs flowers. There's a wine auction. A movie star flies in and needs all white flowers tomorrow morning ASAP. The CEO of a stock brokerage wants twenty bunches of open sunflowers Monday morning before he arrives in town. The grower may be stressed, but so are his clients.

Canal managers deal with big fluctuations in flow by using spills created by prescient builders, who knew that water demands could change quite suddenly—a valley-wide storm might mean no one needs water for a week.

Well before electricity and new technologies emerged to confound the system further, they built large ponds in convenient places for overflows they knew would occur. There, ditch riders could dump excess water when demand quickly lowered, to prevent the canal water turned in days earlier from threatening canal banks.

The canal manager, like the flower grower, faces the task of coordinating hundreds of users' requests so that varying amounts arrive at various times. He calculates how much water to withdraw upstream, how far ahead in time to withdraw it, and how to deal with sudden demand changes. What if it rains? What if several big users' power goes out simultaneously? Doesn't sound much different than growing and marketing flowers, does it.

Canal users make orders the day before they need water, but a flower client has to notify the farmer 60-90 days ahead to make certain she gets what she needs—and, given her clients' whims, she rarely knows of that need that early. The farmer, then, to avoid losing a possible sale, has to prepare for the unknown, guess the future, be willing to take the risk that he's wrong in order that he might be right. That's why large flower wholesalers become the go-to place for designers—they can be depended on in an emergency because they spread their risk over hundreds and thousands of clients and have access to many growers, and though their quality may be lower in some cases, they almost always come through to fill an order. It's just numbers: if one of a thousand clients orders significantly large amounts, likely the other nine hundred-ninety-nine won't, and stocks on hand cover the sudden rise in demand. But if one of a small grower's ten or twenty clients triples demand then either he won't be able to meet it or, if he can meet it, then on weeks when there is no large upswing his product will hit the compost heap.

If you can't stand a colorful compost pile, if you don't have secondary "spills", you face a different problem: if you tighten your supply, you won't meet heavy demand if it arises. And if you consistently fail to meet demand, or even fail once for some clients, your trustworthiness shrinks and your clients look elsewhere. Your business and reputation suffers. I once heard a market farmer remark that he wished he "could be sold out at ten AM and go home", and you might guess from his insight that he never became successful. He was thinking of limiting waste instead of the demand he would miss if he lacked product to sell in those last three hours of market. His was a way of looking at things that cannot lead to success.

Still, no one likes to see their flowers wasted and rotting in the compost, so there are a couple of things you can do to allay that problem. You can't really stop over-raising flowers since you need to make sure you have plenty, but you can try to limit overproduction as best you can—if you have the space to grow extra and a crop is easy to grow, don't skimp on overplanting; guess how much you might sell, add the percentage you're comfortable with tossing without agonizing over your failure. As harvest comes, assess demand and refrain from overcutting as the cooler fills—you'll cuss yourself when you get that late call for ten Baptisia bunches you didn't harvest, but just remember the other twenty times when you cut too much and your labor went to waste, and remember the other times you smartly left flowers in the field rather than harvesting and throwing them away.

One of statistics' primary virtues is admitting mistakes are inevitable, knowing that you always run the risk of either hanging an innocent man or letting a guilty one go free. That's why poll numbers come with a +/- margin of error—pollsters know the data might be off, that they can't be perfect. It's the same for flower growers, who can grow more than they need and always meet demand (and also waste a certain amount of effort), or grow too little and waste nothing but fail to match the demand. You make the choice, you have little chance of hitting the perfect amount, but remember if you don't have it you can't sell it, so the only way you'll ever get that sale is to grow it. The key is to grow too much, but not a whole lot of too much, and that will always be a difficult, maybe impossible, thing to do. Once you realize the only mistake you can make is thinking you have a chance to not make a mistake, it becomes much easier.

IT'S ALL MATH

F LOWER FARMING, IT'S all math—terrifying, eh? It shouldn't terrify you, though, because it doesn't mean you have to be a mathematician. You don't need to know quadratic equations, logarithms, algorithms, or even algebra but you do need to understand more and less—meaning you have to be able to add and subtract. Any other mathematical knowledge you have is gravy.

In all you do on the farm, remember the math. You want less expenses and more income—low input and high output equals a successful farm. If you want, you can put all this on paper, but you should be able to get a feel for it even without the tedium of numbers. It doesn't take a rocket scientist to see it takes too long to cut X flower if you sell it at Y price when you can cut another flower in half the time for the same price. What are your techniques yielding you? You should hone your perception until you see exactly what inputs cost. Price your time, price the wear and tear on your brain—there's a cost to all the thinking you do at night and in winter and you likely aren't including it when you consider all your inputs. You don't have to put a number on it, but you have to be acutely aware of it because nothing matters more than your peace of mind, the joy of farming. If it's a drain, cost it as such.

Remember this in the movement from quality product to perfect product, because the effort between pretty good and excellent likely provides no benefit to you. If effort used from improving A- product to A+ product costs a buck, and product price for A+ is only a buck more, you've really wasted your effort. You need to think of high returns, low input and high output, and extra cost, time or effort that yields only a small amount more just pulls from that finite pool of your resources. Stop trying to be perfect. Cut yourself some slack.

Speaking of slack, make sure you have it everywhere. Slack means possibility and freedom, so take advantage of it when it comes. While you have an electrician around installing power, install extra in case you expand. If you can have extra water available you can take advantage of it during droughts or when you expand. You don't have to use it, it doesn't cost you anything, but it gives you possibilities, it gives you cushion, it should give you peace of mind. If you build a bigger cooler than you need, your business can grow—it doesn't cost as much to go bigger when you build the first time as it does if you add to it later. If you can afford extra land and it's only a small percentage extra, buy it for future use. It's just math, it's bank, padding for a rainy day, a resource you can use as your business grows.

Of course there are limits. If you need a 50 square foot cooler right now, you don't necessarily need to build a 5000 square foot cooler—there's such a thing as too much slack. You may not need a thousand acres, either, or three phase power, or the water rights to five hundred acres. But give yourself some room in all phases of your actions, it's best to have a little extra slack, more freedom and possibilities.

The sales interaction is just math—or maybe it's just geology, since increasing the number of contact points between any two things raises the likelihood of erosion. While it may also be true that increased contact means more symbiotic possibilities, we're going to stick with the Second Law of Thermodynamics, or entropy, which states that while mass can only be changed and not destroyed, it always changes toward disorder rather than order, toward unusable rather than usable. This means that after the first hello to the client, things are more likely to go downhill than not.

You're a nice person, your clients are nice. You charge a fair price, your clients pay you fairly—so why, then, in times of high gas prices, are you tempted to add a surcharge to customers' bills? When your flower buckets don't get returned why are you irked and think to add a bucket charge? Why add a delivery fee, particularly to clients who buy very little? Why, if you ship, do you have the urge to tack on handling fees, box fees, ice fees? Well, because however nice we all are, our needs are different and wherever the client's needs don't match the seller's needs disagreement arises.

Since a certain amount of conflict appears inevitable where two wills collide, we suggest you keep the sales interaction simple. *Don't* add surcharges, *Don't* add bucket charges, *Don't* add fees of any sort. Give the client less reason to think you're out to gouge them. Instead of adding line after line of extra charges, include your costs in your flower prices. Do you add a weeding surcharge on years the weeds are worse? An irrigation surcharge on dry years, an insect management fee on bad bug years? Probably not. Clients don't want or need to know about your increased or decreased costs, they just want to know your price and decide whether to pay it or not. Each extra fee you charge gives them another opportunity to refuse your business—why would you provide an opening to do so?

If you're a small enterprise, keep your pricing simple. The fewer price points you have, the easier it is for both your sales representative (very possibly, you) and the client. The math needed to multiply ten bunches by eight dollars comes easier than the math of five bunches at 7.95, two bunches at 6.95, two at 5.95 and one at 9.95. Again, you're making places for mistakes. Ten times eight is just one problem, while the second example gives four multiplication problems plus one addition problem to bring them together. You don't want your clients to be working out math in their heads, you want them buying, making impulse purchases. Every moment you provide someone is a moment to say no, to think twice, to think again, their firm resolve to buy eroding into *maybe*, then to *maybe next time*, then to an absolute *no*. It may sound like we're trying to convince you to cheat your client, but it's just a way to streamline action. If you play baseball, you know that thinking about a bouncing baseball makes you more inclined to miss it with your mitt, and thinking about a free throw in basketball is a recipe for missing it. Thought tends to complicate action in a way that befuddles it (Camus wrote that "thinking is the first step toward undermining oneself"), so make the client relationship an instinctual one rather than a thoughtful one.

On your website make payment easy. You want cash in your hand as quickly as possible, shrink the time that a customer has to think about the transaction. You're not trying to take advantage, you're just trying to help the client get on with her business.

Always and Never

Always and never are mathematical terms, everyone understands them. Usually, mostly, quite a bit—these are subjective terms that mean different things to different people. You may think *usually* showing up on time to be one thing, the client or the boss thinks it quite another. They remember when you didn't show up, you remember when you did. Maybe you think supplying *most* of the order to be a bang-up job, the client remembers not having that flower she needed for the bridal bouquet. Try to *always* complete orders, *always* show up on time on the same days, *never* be absent from the farm long enough to miss orders. Two things, all or none, are so much easier to deal with than all the possibilities in between.

Pricing and Value

We see a lot of new farmers (and old ones, too) waste time comparing prices, complaining about prices they pay and prices they get, about getting cheated. Freight costs too much from X in comparison to Y, a little job costs as much as a big one when a service man comes. If you've been around kids, you know the syndrome from the playground: *teacher, it's not fair; he's getting more than me.* If you have more than one child, you've heard: *Bobby got a bigger piece than me; Sally's always first.* We're sure you can hear the kids whining now. Hopefully, you catch a memory of yourself whining, too, and immediately recognize something in yourself that remains from childhood, it's a bad appendix. Remove it.

It's hard for us to get over the fact that life isn't fair. There might be something objective called fairness that we might all agree with, but just coming up with those criteria becomes so exhausting that we gladly settle for less.

An offshoot of objective fairness is the notion of value. Value isn't objective, either. There isn't an imaginary, ideal worth of a thing. I had the first issue of Marvel's Silver Surfer comic book, and theoretically it was worth hundreds of dollars, but because I may have been the only comic book collector in three or four counties, it had no worth at all in the context where I existed. Value's an agreement between buyer and seller. The plumber has to drive to your place to change a screen in the faucet and it takes him as long as driving to replace someone else's water heater. To you the first job seems smaller, much smaller, so the cost should be much lower, but to him it takes up time he could be making more money elsewhere. Your measurements aren't his, it's as if you were measuring lengths and he was measuring volume—you're all upset, he's all upset, and you're fighting like monkeys over territory that neither of you own.

If a service or a thing is worth what is asked, get it. If it's not, don't. It's as simple as that. Don't think about fairness, about being cheated or about cheating, just keep it simple: yes or no. Undoubtedly you'll get your panties in a twist from time to time over being undervalued or being overcharged and when you do just remember this lesson and quit acting like you always get the dirty end of the stick.

Don't undervalue your time. If you're on the computer or phone trying to find the best deal and save five bucks on something, realize not only the cost of your time but the wear and tear on your psyche. Something happens to your way of being when you start whittling away and dickering, it turns you miserly, at worst, and at best just wastes your time, gives you habits better spent otherwise, takes up space in your brain better used for something else. You can itemize and monetize the wear and tear on your brain, but we just triple what we think our physical costs are and it seems to come out close to what the rest of the world charges. Using this sloppy equation also saves us the erosion that would happen if we spent time trying to put numbers to worry and stress.

Efficiency

Historians sometimes credit Henry Ford as the assembly line inventor, giving him prominence as the impetus for industrial efficiency. His "discovery"? Complex things (like cars) get built more quickly by having many workers, each doing only one thing, over and over, rather than one worker doing all the things required to build a single car. It's just math—fewer possibilities for mistakes, less time wasted preparing for different tasks or cleaning up after them, no need for re-tooling the brain for another procedure.

You'll find his premise holding true on the farm. If you interrupt what you're doing when you see something else that needs done, you take longer to do the two tasks when you intertwine them than you would if you completed one, then moved to complete the other. When you think about it, it's pretty simple: every task requires preparation, however minute, and every task requires cleanup, however small, and between any two things is a space or a time, that distance varying, depending on the tasks. It may seem that you just as well pull that weed in the neighboring row since you're right there beside it cutting flowers, but it takes a few seconds to gird your loins, move over, pull the weed, move back, reset your brain to what you've been doing. In the short term, it seems like a small thing, but add those things up and at the end of the workday you've shrunk your efficiency.

You don't need to get obsessed about this—sure, if you see a dandelion blooming, by all means pull the head off and even yank the plant since not doing so means letting it go to seed and giving you more work in future years—but if a task you see can wait, let it wait, continue what you're doing. File it away on that long list of "things to do" and it'll surface later in the day or week.

So, it's all math, but it's simple math. That wasn't so hard, was it?

TECHNITIS

I F, WHEN YOU see a new task to be done, you
immediately think of a way to do it better, you may
suffer from technitis, the belief that any problem can be
fixed through technique. The symptoms are:

1) Automatic distraction by the thought of
   improvement—the sufferer, rather than simply
   performing a task, strays off course to create a way
   to do it better. If the task could have been done
   faster than the period it took to stray, you have a
   bad case of the affliction.

2) Automatic belief that you can do it better than the
   way it's been done—if you think you're smarter
   than generations of engineers, you suffer not just
   from technitis but egotism. Maybe, just maybe,
   you do know more, are more able, but likely, the

thousands of hours put in by others surpasses your experience and ability.

3) Involuntary reaction of glee upon seeing an equipment catalog in the mail.

4) An unshakable belief in method. If, when something goes wrong, instead of simply saying "I screwed up" you look for a disruption in your method to blame for the snafu, you have technitis. You are exporting responsibility to a chain in the outside world: the tool wasn't sharp, something distracted you, you skipped a step, someone interrupted you, you were in a hurry. All these reasons might in fact be true, but it's still thinking that the magic lies in a thing, a way, rather than in you, your focus, your skill.

We laugh at pre-scientific era humans because they believed in demons, used magic talismans and performed sacrifices, but take a look at the things sold on afternoon TV: magnetic belts to make you lose weight, exercise equipment you'll never use, things to keep you awake, give you abs, perk up your libido and you'll note we have not come that far down the road to enlightenment. And even in the annals of the learned you see a religious fascination with technology, with "the answer", be it nuclear fusion (let's see, that was just around the corner when I was in the fifth grade in 1966—and it's still just around the corner 150 billion research dollars later), ceramic carburetors, hydrogen-powered cars... Pick up any magazine, scientific or mechanical or New Age and you'll find a bit of magic on the cover aimed at getting you to buy it. Some of the magic actually comes to fruition but most does not.

There's a human frailty that transports us out of the present, and it can go two ways: we can remember a golden age, an Eden, when everything was wonderful, or we can imagine a prophesied utopia where there's no evil, no war, no energy shortage, free food, free shelter and such. If you were a high school quarterback or cheerleader, if you were the center of attention, if you had the perfect childhood, you can create a golden age but you're conveniently forgetting the bad moments, I assure you. And if you extrapolate to some past where everything was in harmony—be it putting indigenous cultures on a pedestal, believing in idylls written in religious texts, or clinging to myths—I assure you, it didn't happen the way you imagine. Life requires movement, nature creates problems in order to generate newness, and where species, climates, individuals collide disorder and pain occur to set the stage for new configurations of being. There may be respites, what the Greeks called *hesuchia*, the moment after the contest, but they don't last long and we, and life, move on to the next conflict.

It all amounts to our need for a quick solution to what might be chronic problems—but what if there isn't a problem at all? Maybe, just maybe, the problem is we see problems where there aren't any.

Many entering flower farming already suffer from technitis. They see someone shoveling a trench and imagine a machine that will do it for them. They tire of transplanting plugs, bending and standing, bending and standing, bending and standing, aching and groaning, and dream of machines to ease the task. There is a time and place for technology, but first you need to be cured of technitis. So ask yourself:

Can the technique or equipment be used in multiple ways at multiple times?

Does it fit the scale of your farm?

Does its cost exceed the profit it will bring?

Does it shrink the chain of actions in a task or make it longer?

Can you recover costs if you sell it?

There are entire industries based on mining your technitis. It may be what the entire economy is based on—after all, aren't stocks just a belief you can get a lot for a little? If you often speak of how much you saved on a deal, particularly on something you didn't need, haven't you been buffaloed by those who recognize your affliction and seize the opportunity: the seller never tells you how much you pay, just how much you save, the bartender doesn't remind you of the hangover, the pusher doesn't remind you of rehab—they all rely on your ability to deny reality.

In our county, where everyone does crafts and no one consequently needs them, you still can sell the idea of *selling* crafts to those who think making a living at what they love might be possible. Classes get filled by those who want an easier route, and if you tell them there's such a way they want to listen. Nationwide, you'll see Florist Design

Schools, Farm Schools, Massage Therapy Schools, Yoga Certification Schools, all charging exorbitant amounts to floods of customers who have a dream they can make it big doing something they like instead of sweeping the junior high school floors. Some people actually come out of these schools and make a go of it, but I bet you know a half dozen with unused "degrees" for every one who succeeded. Magical as any of the mentioned occupations might be, success in the endeavors comes from the additional hard work you bring to them.

It's said if you tie a pencil to a chicken's beak it will be hypnotized and stare at it, try to follow it until it collapses and dies. Hopefully no one's taken the experiment that far, but no doubt most of us will take a similar habit to the grave. NEW! FREE! IMPROVED! The ads get us every time, which is why they're used so often. You probably can't afford a hundred-dollar-an-hour cognitive therapist to retrain you to become averse to these and like words, so you'll need to do it yourself. New doesn't mean better, ever, it just means new. Better means better, new means new. Although sometimes new means "old with a different name." It's a form of technitis, this fascination with the new, so let's work on weaning ourselves off of it.

There's nothing inherently magical about anything, although the world is pretty magical and flowers even more so, but the magic that solves a problem instantly is just in your mind. There've been some pretty good inventions that made life better, like plumbing and electricity and cars, but even those have their drawbacks as the entire planet overuses them. You can't solve every problem with a quick fix, but you can perform a little authentic magic of your own by becoming more efficient, eliminating the bugs in your operation bit by bit. The hard way, not the easy one.

That's why you should steer away from any new kind of TV, a revolutionary car, any new gadget: there hasn't been time to work out the bugs. Believe me, I know, having invested half my life savings in solar power in the seventies, and having bought a windmill a decade ago that won't pay for itself for fifty years (longer, since it's been broken for three years).

It's a difficult thing for flower growers especially, since their business is based on appearance, to understand that appearance is deceiving. It seems counterintuitive, maybe even a bit deceitful, to turn from appearance when you want others to turn toward it.

WEEDS

NOW TO THE child care part of the book, the place to tell you how to establish and maintain boundaries with that naughty, if delightful, impish Nancy Nature who provides so much pleasure and is simultaneously so consternating.

You've seen the deals—free or low price subscription for six months (with automatic renewal at a much higher price); no money down on furniture, interest free for one year (and then, exorbitant rates); low interest credit cards (so long as you pay them off at the end of the month) that have increasing rates after an introductory period. It's a game companies play, a marketing ploy. They know that most people forget to read the fine print and that, even if they do, they pay attention to the first part of the bargain and quickly forget the second.

To the cut flower grower, weeds are nature's fine print. "Look! All these beautiful blooms!" Little Nancy

Nature says, sneaking in a thousand weed seeds under the canopy of Scabiosa foliage. She knows that as you harvest away you won't notice the interest payments coming due. Nature's betting you'll lose, but just as you can win the subscription game by canceling your renewal, just as you can win the credit card game by paying off your bill before interest starts accruing, you can win the weed game with a few techniques that require nothing but your attention and diligence.

What is a weed? (And you thought you knew!)

First of all, there are no weeds.

Secondly, everything is a weed.

Sound contradictory? Not really, because there is no category of plants labeled *weed*—it's just a word we give to a plant we don't want at a particular time in a particular place. Thistles are weeds—until we grow them for cuts (Echinops). Dill, Orach, and feverfew are "good" plants when we grow them for sale as flowers—until they go to seed and cause us headaches for years to come. Then they're weeds. Frosted explosion, a grass in the Panicum group, was a weed that plagued our first acreage so badly that we sometimes abandoned crops, but now we intentionally grow it (in an extremely quarantined spot, watched over with diligence). *Where* a plant is determines its weediness as much as *what* it is, and *when* it goes to seed and *how much* it seeds (or spreads rhizomatously) determines its perniciousness.

It's not that we don't like weeds, it's not that we want to exterminate them from the face of the planet, it's just that they're ill-behaved and don't have good boundaries—if they would just take a portion of nutrients instead of most of them, we'd furnish their needs, and if they just took some space instead of most of it, we'd gladly offer them a home. But it's when they go to seed and overwhelm us that they become our enemy.

We started Bindweed Farm on what may have been the weediest and rockiest ground in the county (if not the world), so we've become, well, phobic toward unwanted plants. We had to hunt for flowers amid the weeds on our first acreage, pull clingy grass seed heads from the Velcro-like stems of Black-eyed Susans, unravel morning glory from flower stems, spending far more time weeding than harvesting. Or planting. Or irrigating. Or tilling. We had to learn a few things and learn them quick.

Timing

It's all about timing. Your intended seeds need to germinate sooner, your wanted plants need to grow faster, and you need to cancel your subscription the minute rates go up—plow any plot under before weeds (and flowers, too) go to seed.

The first rule of weed prevention is to know the conditions needed for your own seeds to germinate. Initially, naïve as we were, we thought that planting our seeds early would give them a lead on weed seeds—HA! As you might imagine, the number of weeds that germinate at low soil temperatures far exceeds the number of flowers that do. Weeds are weeds because they have wide windows: their light requirements are flexible, their temperature needs are undemanding, they grow quickly, vigorously, are opportunistic. Weediness might be defined, actually, as easy to germinate, not fussy about placement, fast-growing, and prolifically seeding.

So pay attention to seed needs—every species has a perfect temperature, a specific light or darkness need, a prime planting depth among other factors at which it germinates best, and if you plant seeds in fifty degree soil when they germinate at sixty degrees you'll give a two week head start to every weed species that germinates between those two temperatures. In fact it's best not to jump the gun and plant the moment your seeds WILL germinate but to wait a bit until they germinate fast. Plant seeds at an appropriate time and you'll give them at least an even chance out of the starting blocks.

Plant Plugs

If you plant slow developing species from seed, your desired crops will inevitably fall behind speedily growing weeds. That's why we never seed perennials and that's why we usually grow even annuals from plugs. Perennials are generally slow growing since they're programmed to seed again and again over many years—they're lumbering work horses, not thoroughbred race horses. Annuals need to get things done if they're going to bloom and fruit before a killing frost occurs, so they come out of the ground raring to grow. Planting perennial plugs, plants already months old, gives them a lead on weeds, and planting annual plugs, usually eight to twelve weeks old, means even fast-growing weeds will have less ability to compete. If you space plugs just an inch or two wider than your weeding implement's width, the most spacey employee can mindlessly hoe his way down the row without even looking by just mechanically swinging between plants.

We direct seed only quick growing annuals like Sunflowers, grasses and Zinnias. They germinate fast, shoot up quickly, dwarf other species. Some early bloomers like Larkspur and Nigella also grow fast enough to compete with weeds and they may actually catch up to plugs planted at the same time.

Know when to give up

If weeds in a crop get ahead of you, give up and put the crop under. A lot of beginning growers, trying to maximize the utility of small areas, keep cutting a plot well after they should. They want to get every dollar they can and it seems that all the work—the planting, the irrigating, the fertilizing, the weeding—has been done, so every extra flower seems like money in the bank. This is where Nancy Nature trips even savvy growers up, because while those "free" flowers keep coming the weedy interest payments surrounding them spread, bud, and go to seed.

In dollar terms, few lengthened harvests from a weed-infested plot make up for the cost of weeding it for years into the future. Some weeds produce a half million seeds per plant, so letting them mature in order to net a couple hundred dollars becomes a monetary loss that may run into thousands of dollars in the long run.

Every cut flower species has a rising curve that begins with a few blooms to cut and swells to hundreds or thousands a day, depending on the size of your plot, and at the same time every plot of ground has a rising curve of weed growth that begins at zero when you plant in virgin soil and rapidly expands as temperatures warm and laborers fail at their weeding jobs. The harvest curve should always be ahead of the weed curve, and when that harvest curve starts falling its weedy counterpart continues to rise: putting the crop down as the harvest curve drops below the weed curve is a good rule of thumb, as weeds generally start budding well before you see their growth slow.

Other Techniques

Techniques for weed control include the manual, the mechanical, and the chemical. Generally, you need to handle any method as Lao-Tse would, judging by what he wrote about how governments should operate: "rule the people as you would fry a small fish." Meaning: tread lightly, use only as needed. This means no recreational tilling, no spraying more than the minimum.

Chemical Means

It's not unusual to see local small landowners and even county weed departments spraying weedkiller on waste areas and roadsides well past the point of the chemical's usefulness. It must make them feel good when they see the results of their labor a few days later, but the browned and wilted foliage doesn't mean what they think it does. Sure, they've halted growth, but any weeds already in the bud stage continue to make seed so they're just wasting time. Spray early in the life cycle or don't spray at all.

Spring blooming weeds like cheatgrass and hornseed require attention well before frosts cease, or they'll just go on down the path to proliferation. Dandelions and thistles need to be hit extra hard well before bud stage to prevent seeding. Pay attention to when your perennial plants emerge and spray the area just before they do so, as the first crops of weeds likely precede them. Eye early emergers like peonies and if you see no shoots, spray. You won't get another chance. Asclepias, Balloonflower and other late risers are candidates for late spraying, so you can withhold the early patrols through the field if your timing is perfect. Use a drift guard on your spray wand—one looking much like those put on dogs after surgery, to focus spray. This allows you to work close to shrubs and other plants, spray even in light winds, and spot spray single plants. Don't spray after recent rain, if there's a heavy dew, or if forecasts suggest rain. Water on the plant dilutes the spray, and rain will wash it off. Most herbicides require a couple hours to fully integrate into the plant's system and damage it severely enough to kill. The younger the plant the more easy it is to kill with spray; there's no point in spraying mature annuals that are going to seed. Don't spray in windy conditions, watch the spray pattern to determine how much a breeze affects it, lower or raise the wand accordingly, adjust the pressure to minimize drift. Heavy droplets carry less far, so lower the pressure as breezes increase.

The non-organic grower possesses a greater arsenal of tools than his counterparts, having 2-4-D, a broadleaf weed killer that can, if used properly, be used on grasses without killing them, Poast and related selective grass-killing chemicals that can (again, if used properly) be sprayed over broadleaf crops without killing them, and Glyphosate, an all around killer that works on most everything except the most pernicious species. There are sterilants, probably not a good choice in any but the most dire circumstance, and numerous chemicals with very specific foci like thistles and evergreens. Most chemicals work because plants draw the chemical in, so young, healthy plants are more likely to imbibe a spray while old, toughened ones have ceased growing and those near or past the bud stage can continue making seed even after being sprayed.

Even if you embrace chemical use, there's no reason to be excessive. Don't overspray, don't overuse.

Mechanical means work well for open areas, and skilled operators can become pretty adept at tilling closely to crops—though even the skilled sometimes generate what farmers call "cultivator blight", a euphemism for the effects of a too-aggressive tractor driver. Rotovators, discs, cultivator shovels and other attachments effectively destroy weeds between rows and on ends of fields.

If you decide on mechanical means, you need a system of sorts. Whatever the width of your tractor determines the width of your equipment which in turn determines the width of your rows—you need to be able to till aisles, so they need to be as wide as the tractor, and you need to cultivate rows, so they have to be between the wheel paths. Take some measurements, outside of one tire to outside of the other, center to center, inside to inside. Your implements should cover outside to outside—if it's sixty inches, buy a sixty inch tiller so that it covers the wheel tracks. Your center to center measurement determines where other tilling instruments will be, whether they be tines or v-shaped duckfeet. These will be attached to a toolbar, an essential and cheap implement that allows you to attach tools—cultivators, drip tape shanks, or other items—wherever you wish. If you clamp duck feet immediately behind the centers of the tires, and if they're the correct width, they will cultivate the tire tracks out and remove weeds in them. The inside to inside measurement gives you how much space you have for plants—you can have one row, two, three or even four, depending on your tractor width, but you need to keep them consistent with your system. We have two rows, eighteen inches apart, centered behind the tractor, but you could have closer rows or wider or even just one, depending on your plant species and your wishes. Once you've determined the row spacing, you can purchase whatever width of tilling instrument you want. Since uneven terrain and inattentive tractor driver results in variable cultivating, we put a little slack in our system to allow for mistakes and drawbar arm swing. Thus, our cultivating shanks are at least a couple inches narrower than the distance between planted rows, so the tractor driver can rock out or text his girlfriend without doing too much damage. But if you're pretty proud of your driving ability you can tighten up your cultivation by widening your tilling shanks until they begin inducing cultivator blight.

There's a wide array of weeding tools for tractors, some we've not been brave enough to use but have seen in impressive action, but we've stayed with the simplest—a rotovator for aisles and open areas, in addition to putting crops under, and duckfeet to run shallowly between the rows.

Manual Means

Scuffle hoes, AKA hoop hoes or stirrup hoes, work best for manual work on smaller weeds, as they cut below the surface without disturbing the soil as standard hoes do (disturbing the soil brings new seeds to the surface to germinate). Scuffle hoes create a shallow surface layer of soil that dries out quickly, basically providing a "mulch" of dust that keeps new seeds from growing. The wheel hoe is a scuffle hoe attached to a pneumatic tire (steel wheeled scuffle hoes, in our experience, are much harder to use).

If you're in shape you can weed an acre an hour with a wheel hoe once you get the feel of using it. Wire weeders are good hand tools that can work close to drip tape without damaging it, and the L-shaped elbow hoe is a fine implement that can be placed right up against the stem of a plant and rotated outward to remove close weeds. If you miss weeds the first time around with these tools you might need to use the regular, chopping blade hoe, and tap rooted weeds like dandelions or field geranium may require a soil knife to reach deep into the soil. If you bury drip tape to irrigate, you'll find it a real trick to get a taproot without damaging drip tape, so don't cut too deep beneath the soil.

Any piece of taproot left in the ground will just continue to grow, so soil knives and chopping hoes often just delay weed growth rather than eliminating the problem completely, but remember, it's not the weed itself but the weed going to seed that is the problem, so if you have to come back in a month and dig out a dandelion again, well, that's better than leaving it to go to seed and digging out a thousand next year and a hundred thousand the year after.

Again, some growers even restrict themselves from hoes and other manual means, aiming for the least impactful method of weed control: no-till or permaculture. These methods hearken to the notion that a wise farmer with a deft and light hand can manipulate nature to provide desired ends with minimal but clever means. No-till users generally benefit from moist climates and soils with high humus content that hasten the deterioration of surface vegetation, and they hasten it further with the use of synthetic ground covers that up the rotting effects of the environment. Then, after pulling the covers off when the vegetation has incorporated back into the earth, they add compost and micronutrients over the rotted material and plant right into the manufactured soil without tilling.

If you choose this route, remember you're choosing the most difficult of methods and again, blame no one but yourself for failure—and give no one but yourself credit for success, if you do indeed succeed. Many beginners start with permaculture or no-till intentions because the ideas behind them seem quite enticing: a near zero impact on the environment. Nonetheless, these are methods for experts, not beginners. Just as seeing an overwhelmingly beautiful painting might inspire you to begin painting, or just as seeing a skilled Olympic gymnast might make you aim to become one yourself, seeing a seasoned farmer who has refined his techniques and shaped his farm into a low-impact operation might make you want to emulate him. If you've ever succumbed to such hero worship, be it toward painters, musicians, athletes, writers or any accomplished artist or worker, and began to step down the path toward matching them, you'll know the foolishness of doing so. There are a lot of steps between a paint-by-numberist and a Picasso— don't get ahead of yourself.

Timing—deadheading

Your desired crops can quickly become weeds, so deadhead blooms before they seed. Some crops are far worse than others, with Phlox no problem at all for us but Matricaria, Orach, Dill, grasses and most annuals being notorious for showing up where they don't belong if left to go to seed. When we try to eke out another day of cutting instead of hitching up the rotovator to put the crop under, we know we may be making a mistake—we're not much different from the dieter who says "one more piece of pie can't hurt."

Anything used as a pod or seedhead particularly poses danger, being closer to seed than bloom, so beware of waiting too long to harvest Nigella pods, Belamcanda lilies, Atriplex, and other species with attractive end-of-life states. Even if you practice diligence and harvest the moment it's possible, you'll likely still have a minor problem when harvesting plants at this stage.

Controlling invasive species

Sometimes you just can't resist planting an invasive species because your clientele loves it. Silver King and Mints are jus a couple species that can quickly ruin neighboring plots if left uncontrolled, even in desert climates like ours. If you really can't resist planting such threats, leave wide spaces around them so you can till or spray with chemicals to keep them at bay.

Mulching and cover crops

Anything you can do to deprive weeds of habitat helps you as a grower. Mulching open areas keeps most weeds from growing, though perennials like quackgrass and bindweed work their way easily through even thickly applied mulch. These crops, and any rhizomatous plant, continue to grow if covered by landscape fabric or plastic, since they send out scout roots to find the edge of the covering matter, then send up shoots to the open surface to begin growing again. Beware of mulch, however, as it may contain weed seeds if produced in improper conditions, and "free" wood chips gleaned from landscapers often includes material from species that easily regrow from even small pieces. We pulled Russian Olive saplings for years, thanks to a few free loads of chips from a tree trimming service, and yanked willows from greenhouse paths even five years after application, not knowing just how vigorous some species are.

Many perennial crops, and some annuals, can be mulched to prevent weed growth. All can be surrounded by mulch, though central stems of some species may be susceptible to fungal or bacterial diseases in the enhanced microclimate, but those with taproots which put leaves on along a stem, rather than growing a rosette, respond well to heavy mulching right over the top if the mulch is applied before the stem comes through the ground in the spring. These include Asclepias and Baptisia, while Scabiosa, Penstemons and the like that put their leaves on close to the ground can't really be covered without depriving the leaves of sunlight (and also inspiring fungal and disease growth).

Some growers use cover crops under the principle "where a rose grows, there a weed does not", and no doubt this works to some extent. But beware of this method, too, as anything other than smooth, barren ground provides a place for weed seeds to gather when wind currents deposit their load. If you have a wind barrier, you'll notice that on the lee side weeds may be worse, as the energy of a current lessens there enough that it can't carry as much. If you're a gold panner, you'll know this works with water, too, as heavy particles like gold drop behind rocks and other impediments in a stream. And cover crop leaves provide a perfect net to catch light seeds like salsify or dandelions. Once a canopy appears, weeding becomes impossible in a cover cropped area, so choose quick growing species, preferably those that germinate at times your prevalent weed species don't. Lastly, improperly managed cover crops can themselves go to seed and become longterm problems. Covers prevent weed growth, but can also inspire it. Your situation will determine which they do more.

Weeding dos and don'ts

Every crevice, hump, dip, or dirt clod provides habitat for weed seed dropped by wind currents. The change in terrain offers change in conditions: extra shade, additional moisture, protection from foragers all boost weed seeds' probability of success. Any change in the surface alters a wind current's path and energy, so the larger the rise in terrain the more likely seeds and other debris will drop on the lee side.

When you plant, remember any empty space offers a place for weeds to grow, so plant as close as you can so that *your* plant chokes out and inhibits others. Plant at a width allowing your chosen implements free access to do their jobs—if your tractor is four feet wide, make your walkways four feet wide so they can be tilled or mowed; make your rows so that cultivating shovels can be pulled behind the wheels to eradicate weeds and additional shovels can fit between the rows; if your scuffle hoe is six inches wide, plant eight inches apart so the hoe moves easily through the open space.

Each time you go through a plot you miss a few weeds—it's inevitable. We used to get angry when an employee left obvious weeds until we measured our own performances. Some weeds evade the eye from one side of the row and not the other, some match the soil's color, and some possess leaf shape so similar to its companion plant (like dandelions do with Scabiosa) that only very skillful weeders can spot them (who knew the intricacies required for such menial tasks).

As the season progresses your mistakes accumulate. Even if you're 99% efficient, you're missing one percent of the weeds, and each week that one percent adds to the previous weeks' one percents, until weeds overrun the plot. It's like relationships—first loves are perfect, until they're not. Once a first misunderstanding takes place (she squeezes the toothpaste in the middle of the tube!) the love begins to deteriorate, and as mistakes accumulate the memories of being wronged (or wronging) and distasteful differences overwhelm the easy flow of total infatuation. Memories can't be wiped away, but luckily mistakenly left weeds can be eradicated, so you can fix the flower bed as you can't your perfect love.

But even the most diligent of us eventually get overwhelmed by the sheer enormity of our mistakes piling up on each other, and when this happens its time to put a bed under, plow under weeds and flowers alike, before they bud. Since many, if not most, plants continue to form seed once in bud, even when ripped from the ground or sprayed with chemical, it's crucial to take care of the problem long before most of us normally consider doing so.

If you do wait too long, always pull buds off weed stems whether you pull them from the ground, spray them, or plow them under, as buds continue to get energy and nutrients from the supporting stem tissue, giving them the ability to finish the seeding process.

The weed curve

Perennial crops like peonies can withstand some weed pressure, but even perennials can get so infested that planting a new patch becomes smarter than constantly fighting weeds. The slope of the perennial harvest curve lies flatter than the annual counterpart, it extends over many years rather than a single season, but a perennial flower bed has to contend with two weed curves—the annual weed curve, which annual beds also fight, but also the perennial weed curve that annual beds avoid since they can be plowed after a single short season. Annual weeds respond more easily to weeding in perennials since aged plants can take rougher treatment from a mistakenly aimed hoe, but they're also more difficult to see once canopies develop late in the season. And perennial weeds, once missed because of that canopy, may be impossible to remove if they situate themselves where removal means death to its host.

Acquaint yourself with the pace of weed growth. Be prepared to plant new perennial beds of a particular species a year ahead of when you plan to put the current bed down so you have continuous harvest across the years. Remember, labor costs, whether in deadheading or weeding, cut into profits, and while it's easy to register earnings from harvests those numbers need to be weighed against the extra hours a weedy bed takes.

Mistakes weeders make

We're pretty sure some aspects of weeding reveal a genetic mutation heretofore unknown to science. For instance, almost all laborers, as they near a row's end, lose either their ability to see weeds or their desire to remove them. It's universal!

Then, there's the completely invisible species, the kinds

of weeds no one, whether they've been around gardens or never been out of their video game basement, pulls. Milkweed, for instance, though its distinctly shaped, gray leaves tower above a canopy of neighboring flowers, evades everyone. Piss Elms, obviously not in a row, obviously not a flower, get to stay, as do Poplars, until they grow so tall a backhoe needs to be called in. You can avoid these genetic defects if you tell your laborers to look for *differences*: if it's not in a row, if there aren't many evenly spaced plants matching it, PULL IT! Beware, however, and stick around as employees work, as we once told an employee exactly this and she reversed the order, pulling only the desired Bells of Ireland and none of the weeds.

Another universal mistake: avoiding weeds close to transplants. We don't think we're ogres, we don't jump on our employees when they make a mistake, but still they seem to fear damaging plants and so avoid pulling weeds in close proximity. Okay, sometimes two plants together may be easy to miss—but, come on, not really, they're differently shaped. Maybe the employee's waiting until the weeds get bigger and are easier to pull—but that's not true, they just get more difficult to pull. These weeds are the most important to remove, before their roots get entwined with the flower, after which both weed and transplant eventually will need to be destroyed. So if the weeder wants to avoid hurting plants, his choices are this: wait, and for sure destroy the plant, or try to get it now, and have a chance of the plant surviving. Hold the transplant down with one hand, work your other hand's fingers into the weed's root nearby and pull. Simple.

Deadheading is a form of weeding

Most growers think of deadheading primarily as a way to fool plants into making new buds, but more important, perhaps, is the technique's role of weed prevention—for every flower that goes to seed makes a bed more difficult to manage in subsequent years.

Flower seeds range widely in size, from half a million an ounce to a hundred or less. A single flower head sports hundreds, if not thousands, of seeds, so every blossom left drops enough offspring to carpet the ground in the coming seasons. Even though you consider the species a "good" one, if you don't deadhead you may end up thinking it a "bad" one.

Don't stack your mistakes. It's like not paying your credit card debt down—suddenly, you're paying not just the principal and the interest on the principal, but interest on the interest plus interest plus principal, ad infinitum.

When to weed

Always.

If you ever run out things to do on a farm (admittedly unlikely) you can always weed. But there are times when you may be wasting your time, other times when weeding is easier.

Anytime works for mature weeds with major roots. Yank deep rooted dandelions and field geranium whenever you can, starting as soon as the ground thaws. These pull most easily, of course, in moist ground and may not yield their grip on the earth at all in dry soil. You may find weeding easiest in wet soil, but beware: many weed species re-root if left on wet earth, so make sure the sun's out or the wind's up to dry the exposed roots and keep them from resurrecting. Lore here has it that you can leave quackgrass roots out in the sun on a fence post for a month and still replant it.

You should show restraint even when using mechanical means. A wheel hoe pass through moist soil may do nothing more than provide a momentary break in a weed's day, since gravity brings the soil above back to the soil below and no air pockets exist to dry out the broken roots.

Again, it's the Goldilocks Problem: too wet, too dry, just right. Our first farm had a very narrow window during which we could weed, the soil being composed of the same ingredients as cement and acting much the same. Too wet to weed immediately after irrigation, in twenty four hours it might be too dry to break with a hoe. Find the parameters of your soil and work within the time framework it gives you.

Specific weeds

You can divide weeds into annuals and perennials, but we like to categorize them as acute or chronic pests, the former being sudden bloomers and spreaders that require immediate control and the chronic as being slow growers that give you plenty of time to work on them but are a real beast to control.

Chronic weeds:

Bryony: A recent introduction to our area, appearing only in the last thirty years, this vine can grow a couple feet a day when mature. It might be called the "Kudzu of the West", forming a tuber that may weigh pounds that gives it a storehouse of energy defying even chemical control. Though you can inject the tuber with chemical through a syringe, if you're going to go through that much trouble you just as well dig it out. Be sure to get the entire tuber—any piece that remains in the ground just continues to grow. A lover of fencelines, trees and shrubs, where birds love to plant it when defecating the seeds.

Dandelion: Though dandelions are hard to get rid of they're also easily controlled—an oxymoron, seemingly, but since they only bloom in cool weather (well, almost—once in a while you'll see a flower even in the dead of summer) you only have to be wholly vigilant for that period of time, which lasts about two weeks in May here. During that crucial time we do a daily "dandelion patrol", scouting specifically for dandelions since they might bloom and go to seed in a single day. Yank the head off, making sure no stem remains on the bud in order to deprive it of the strength to seed, then dig as much of it out as possible—if you leave any root, it will grow again, but at least it won't bloom until next year.

Since dandelions insist on being pesky, we scour the field for them as soon as the ground thaws, our soil knives in hand. We return every week to check our inevitable mistakes since they're easily missed, being crown-forming with leaves that emulate those of many flowers. We know we can't completely eliminate them but the constant attention keeps them at bay.

Small specimens pull easily, but dandelions don't need to be very mature before they've sent a taproot too deep to fully remove (at least in our clay soil). Nonetheless, even getting out most of the root sets the plant back a month or two, after which we find it again and perform another amputation—and again and again, many times, until a bed finally gets plowed under.

Morning glory: For the seventy-fifth year in a row, field bindweed took the trophy for most difficult weed to control, as even fumigating the soil sometimes fails to kill it. Chemical experts claim that spraying heavy doses of glyphosate as it flowers works, but in our experience this holds only partly true. If bindweed invades your property, you won't be able to raise late blooming perennials, as the vine quickly overtakes them. Tilling just spreads the rhizomatous roots, so check your implements after passing through infested ground and remove them so you don't spread the problem.

Nightshade: Not the worst weed in the world here, it still clings tenaciously once it's gained a foothold. It's a sneaky one because you think it's not much of a problem so pass it by, then it goes to seed and spreads without you even knowing it.

Quackgrass: Both glyphosate and Poast-like products control quackgrass easily, but if you insist on organic control you have a long career ahead of you since it grows via rhizome. Our suggestion: cave once to your lesser instincts and spray, because once you've taken care of it completely, with a little diligence you'll never have to spray again.

Field geranium: Possibly the champion of taprooted species, sporting a root as thick as a carrot sometimes that reaches feet long (bindweed can reach dozens of feet downward into the soil but its roots cannot match the geranium's thickness), field geranium takes a chemical punch that often just delays its growth. Pull this weed early in its life or face its presence for many years to come. It seeds fairly prolifically—after five years of tillage on one of our new properties, a well-timed rainstorm of sufficient rain at amenable temperatures still brings a carpet of new seedlings to till under.

Canadian thistle: Many thistles, while being heavy seeders, yield to control quite well—particularly crown types easily removed with a little shovel work. But this species grows rhizomatously so digging just excites it, and only specific chemicals designed for it alone work well against it—though a very heavy dose of glyphosate sometimes does the job. Tillage just spreads it, and late spraying won't keep it from seeding out and causing further headaches in the future.

Acute weeds:

Sowthistle: Sowthistle gives you only two opportunities to pull its root—as a very young seedling and as an almost-seeding mature plant. Pulling anytime between these two moments results in breaking off the root, resulting in the plant stooling out to produce even more shoots and blooms. If you miss the crucial early stage, be prepared to go on sowthistle patrol when bloom time rolls around, because it takes only a day for sowthistle to move from bloom to seed. Pull the heads off, making sure not give them any stem to draw sustenance from or they'll continue to mature and make seed, and keep making the rounds every day so that next year you don't have to.

Wood sorrel: We never saw this plant until we left it in a tray we purchased from a reputable nursery from out of state. We thought it was cool looking and didn't even consider it possible that major nurseries might ship weeds out. What a mistake. Now we can't get rid of it in the greenhouses and it's moving into the fields. Though a ground clinger it still presents a problem as an invader, more because it seeds prolifically and offends our aesthetic sensibility, not to mention being somewhat of an upstart challenging our ownership and control. It needs to be taken care of early, frequently, constantly, and you still may never get rid of it because it hides beneath canopies, has a color too dark to see and which often matches the soil.

Chinese lettuce: you'll need gloves for this one, but at least it's forgiving timewise. Pulls easily, is slow to mature, but don't let that lull you into complacency.

Salsify: Also called "oyster plant" since the root purportedly tastes like oysters, this weed's root fetches ten or more dollars a pound in the Whole Foods Market but you won't want it in your field. Make sure to pull the heads off when you remove this from the ground, as it mimics the dandelion not only in its airy seedhead formation but in its ability to draw energy from the stem for further maturation.

Purslane: The worst advice ever given on an organic farming website was to use purslane as a ground cover in order to keep soil cool. Take that advice and you'll be pulling purslane for decades. It seeds prolifically, and the period of time between bloom and seed rivals the dandelion—and because the bloom is tiny and insignificant you may miss the moment completely. It won't get in the way of harvest since it grows low to the ground, but it can choke out competitors and be a liability in terms of fertilizer use.

Panicum elegans: Plant this, also called Frosted Explosion, only if you trust yourself to follow the protocol of weed control. You should harvest it as it nears seed production but you cannot wait until you see seeds as any left in the field will be left for years to come. Harvest, dig, remove, destroy.

Hornseed: Another small ground clinger, easily missed in the spring, really more of a danger for the spiny seeds it sets that get in shoes and socks and tires than for its intrusion into the flower crop.

Buckwheat: You can tell a weeder's an amateur when he mistakes buckwheat (the weed version, not the grain type) for morning glory. We did when we first began farming. At first glance, they both possess heart shaped leaves and both are ground clinging vines, but buckwheat grows faster, is flimsier and has a thinner stem, so once you note the differences you shouldn't mistake them—though if you do, you might just have a weeding disability. Buckwheat seeds fairly prolifically, don't let it get ahead of you.

Knotweed: Another weed many of the help mistakes as bindweed. We tell weeders to let the bindweed go, since we have so little of it and we like to treat it with chemical, so most of them leave this thin stemmed, small leaved ground clinger, too. Not a particularly difficult weed to manage, nor is it very intrusive, but if you're cleaning the kitchen counter, shouldn't you wipe off ALL the crumbs?

Vinegar or other acid products may kill surface

vegetation, but any plant with a root system possessing stored energy will just retaliate. Crop oils actually work better to smother the vegetation of weaker perennial plants.

A quick typology of weeders:

The best weeder works fast, efficiently, mindlessly. The next best works slow, efficiently, mindlessly. Instead, you'll likely find one of the following:

The Coaster: weeds fine until he gets to the end of the row.

The Phoner: weeds fine but has gaps that perfectly correlate to where he was when he got on his phone—more research needs to be done on the effect of phones on vision.

The Pretender: walks down the rows, turns his head back and forth, looks like he's working but does nothing.

The Chopper: sees the weeds, hoes the weeds, but doesn't get rid of the weeds. Instead, he chop the tops off so they make bushier plants in the coming weeks. Job security, one might suppose.

When weeding, look not for weeds but for difference, we tell our workers (not that they listen). We plant a single species in a pretty straight row and anything different that that species, remove. But for most people it's not so easy, instead it's like looking for the gum you dropped in the chicken coop—everything looks the same. When they fail, when we correct them, they do just the opposite of what they should do: they go slower, look more intently, when they should be trying less hard, not harder, stop looking so much and just SEE. Everyone has a speed at which their brain will do the perfect job for them, if they just let it. Read "Zen and the Art of Archery" by Eugen Herrigel and you'll get a better description of the proper way to not just be an archer but to weed. There's a sweet spot in one's attention where your mind neither wanders nor over-focuses, a pace at which your success rate may not reach perfection but comes pretty close. Forget the weeds for a moment when you start, find that pace, you may even start enjoying the work you once found to be drudgery.

CUTTING FLOWERS

━━━━━━━━━❧⟡❧━━━━━━━━━

YOU MIGHT THINK cutting to be a brainless activity that anyone can do. And true enough, anyone can do it—badly. But cutting flowers efficiently, quickly and uniformly approaches artistry. It's just like anything else, you're bad until you're good, then you're so good you forget how bad you were and how difficult it was.

First off, you have to know when a flower is prime to cut. If you grow ninety species, you may need to know ninety different stages of growth. Or worse, if you grow peonies, just one species, you need to know when each variety is best picked, since singles forgive early cutting and doubles may very well not. Not to mention the effect of weather—an ill-timed frost throws everything off, so even if you know when Red Charm should be cut in a normal year, when it gets frozen you need to test every bud to make sure it hasn't been so damaged it will never open. Then there's the heat's effect—on cool days the early blooming Coral Charm won't open as quickly as when the days are sunny and warm, so you must wait longer when it's cool than when it's warm or you may be selling buds instead of flowers.

Every species acts a bit differently, with some best harvested in bud stage and some requiring harvest when fully formed. Zinnias and all Asclepias species, for instance, cease opening once cut, so what you see as you harvest is what you'll see all the way down the cut flower pipeline, clear to the bridal bouquet. Cosmos and Monarda, on the other hand, open even if cut quite tight, so you can open them slowly in the cooler to meet your customers' needs. To confuse matters further, if you cut for a local market you want more open blooms, whereas if you cut for wholesalers you want to cut as early as possible so your buyer has more time to hold your product.

Stem length is important—just as you can cut a twenty foot 2 x 4 into any shorter length you wish, you can cut a long stem shorter, but you can't make either the eight foot 2 x 4 or short stem longer. It's just math—there are more options with a long stem, and you may cringe when you see the three foot sunflower cut to six inches and put in a coffee cup but you just have to give it up.

But stem length isn't as crucial as the first wholesaler we sold to claimed, because many—if not most—flowers go into table arrangements, short bouquets and even boutonnieres. We've sold six inch forget-me-nots and horehound just as short. Still, if you can cut long, cut long, but not so long that you can't transport it. There's no need for eight foot sunflower stems—except when the customer asks for them.

Ideally, every stem in a bunch is the same length, and every bunch of a species should be similarly long. The further up the commercial chain you sell the more exact you'll need to be, but even if you sell only locally your stems should be relatively equal in length. It just makes for easy judgment by the client. At first, cutting similarly lengthy stems may be difficult—some cutters make a mental mark on their forearm or bicep to give them an idea of where to cut. If you need to do this, you'll always be slow because you're putting an extra step into the process. Look at a ruler or make a mark in the dirt, eighteen inches long, twelve inches long, thirty inches long—you just hold that distance in mind and keep it as a "jig" there to conform to each time you cut. You need this ability when cutting and when transplanting, too—eight inch spacing, twelve inch spacing, twenty four inch spacing—because measuring each time you transplant or cut slows the process down. Maybe you're afraid of making a mistake because some prior authority figure embarrassed or berated you—give it up, they aren't around anymore. You need to cut, the boss trusts you, it's okay to make a mistake. If the stems come in too long, they can be trimmed and you can adjust the next cut, if you cut them too short, well, that's a problem, but the next bunch can be longer. It's Goldilocks, it's feedback: cut long, cut short, cut just right, and over time it becomes calibrated memory.

Trust your brain when you cut. It sifts through a

gazillion bits of information a second, organizes it, compresses it into a manageable amount for you to work with, so train it a few times by telling it what stage, what length, what quality, then turn it loose and attend to the counting of stems.

Counting—that's another story. Some people are born counters. I sometimes catch myself as I'm going to sleep, saying 57, 58, 59, or when I'm walking, counting my steps 19, 20, 21—it may be from too much exposure to arithmetic in grade school, but maybe it's genetic. If you can't count as you cut, you'll be at a disadvantage because you need to stop cutting to count your stems to make a bunch while your counting cohort is starting on the next bundle.

Bunching varies from species to species, too. Generally ten stems make a bunch, but woody stems (hydrangeas, viburnums and the like) and peonies generally take five. If you sell in a local market you can make whatever size bunch you want, so long as your clients know the stem count and you keep it consistent. With non-uniform species, like delphiniums, we state on our availability list that 5-8 stems make a bunch, since not only the height varies considerably from stem to stem but the squattiness of flowers on the stem makes for different uses. On these sorts of "mixed" bunches, clients often start specifying whether they want tall or short before ordering—and often they prefer short delphiniums to long ones because they find them more usable.

Bunch cutting

"What's a bunch?" people ask, when they see something on our availability list that we sell not in number of stems but as field bunches. How big is it? Well, it's as big as you want to make it. It's your business, after all.

Typically, the industry defines a field bunch as that which fits inside an average-sized man's first finger and his thumb. This definition holds for most bunch-cut species but changes when you get to something like Heuchera, a flower with such tiny stems that it might take you a half hour to cut a bunch of that size. For species that don't fit the general sizing rule, you just judge how big you can make your own bunches and a) sell them and b) make a profit. See how fast you can cut a bunch in relation to other cutting and decide from there. If someone doesn't want to buy your bunch, thinking it too small, move on to the next client, and if that client thinks it too small, quit growing that flower.

When you bunch cut, find the cutting instrument most comfortable to you. Felco pruners work best on grasses for us, but on some species with less rigid stems we return to the old bonsai scissors. Silver King and sage tend to crimp rather than cut with the Felcos. To bunch cut, just grab a bunch with your first finger and thumb and cut below the grasp, giving yourself the height you desire. For some species, like Alchemilla, this will be near ground level, but for tall things like grasses you'll want to edge your way up until you get to the length you feel your clients want.

Bunching takes the counting work out of cutting. It takes the deciding part out, too, for the most part, as it shouldn't be too hard for even the greenest employee to tell the difference between a marketable bunch and one that's marred (though we had an employee that, rather than omitting dead foliage, added more to the bunch to make up for it). And you can streamline the sleeving part of processing, too, in the bunch cutting of some species. You can stick your hand through a sleeve in the field when cutting Bells of Ireland, for instance—cut a bunch, then pull it through the sleeve with the hand already holding the bunch. Just make sure there's no dew on the plant when you bunch cut and sleeve at the same time, or you'll create a terrarium ripe for fungal problems once the product reaches the cooler.

We bunch cut Matricaria, Catmint, anything that blooms somewhat uniformly but which slows down the process if cut by the single stem. This makes more work for designers since they need to do your job of separating usable from unusable stems, but it also gives them more product with more variability which gives them more value if they're making unique creations.

Deadheading

Every species has its own cutting season. Cloned species tend to be more uniform so are easier to harvest since every plant is a carbon copy of its neighbor. That's why Idaho potato growers started heavy production of the

Norkota variety, which packs an almost perfect potato that requires little sorting, and dropped growing as many Russet Burbanks, a much better, more usable, more storable potato but much more difficult to sort.

Cultivars grown from seed possess more variability—the larger the number of seeds, the wider variability of bloom time, the more possibilities of deformities, the greater chance of throwing differently sized and shaped blooms. And that's just within a species—from species to species even greater differences occur.

Though every species differs, general rules for cutting persist across the board. Take Scabiosa Fama, for instance. A bed of 200 plants. Early in the spring, having made it through its first winter, it may start blooming in May here but these early flowers are short and deformed. Though unusable, these need to be deadheaded and discarded, just to let the plant know its work isn't done, that it needs to make more blooms. The deadheading procedure becomes more important for the later harvest, because any unusable bloom just gets in the way of the harvester. Just think what the interstates would look like if we left broken cars on it, or what our closets would look like if we kept every old piece of clothing (maybe some of your closets DO look like this), what our streets probably looked like before cars when dead horses were left to rot. Leaving mistakes in the way impedes any current activity. When we cut flowers, we want to do it speedily, so every deformed bloom, diseased bloom, spent bloom, short stem, crooked stem, just gets in the way, takes up our time, slowing us down and shrinking our profitability.

As our Scabiosa bed comes into bloom in June, a much greater percentage of blooms prove usable. The early market shows greater demand, the thirst for a flower unseen for many months driving the quest for novelty. We sell every flower we cut, and as we move down the bed we deadhead what few unusable blooms show up so they don't impede later harvests. Every day we repeat the process, but as the days warm and the Scabiosa blooms more prolifically, we reach a market saturation point—we can't sell all the flowers, so we have to deadhead not only bad flowers but good ones since these will start going to seed and will get in the way. You may think you should harvest all the good flowers, just in case you might sell them, but after doing so a few times you'll realize you're wasting your time when you throw the unsold bunches into the compost heap. Take a guess how many bunches you'll sell, cut a few extra in case you're wrong, just deadhead the rest so you're not wasting time grabbing, bunching and counting and taking space up in the cooler.

If your market demand doesn't rise synchronously with the proliferation of blooms, inevitably there'll come a time when you're deadheading more than you're harvesting, so you'll have to decide when to abandon the bed since the time spent per bunch is lessening profitability. This will differ for each individual's taste and ability, but there is an objective place where the cost of keeping up a bed exceeds the profit it earns. You need to abandon it way before that time. Some species you'll till under when they reach that point, some you'll just mow to the crown to prevent seeding and inspire new growth.

Some species with stiff and regular stems, like Eremerus and Allium, need a rubber band not just above where you cut but also below their heads. This makes moving them more manageable without damage. Slide the first rubber band up the stems, then wrap the bottom. You don't even have to sleeve unless you want to give the flowers further protection.

Stripping

Industry standards tell the grower to strip the stems but if you move your flowers quickly from field to client you may not need to. If the flowers don't sit long enough for bacteria to work the extra foliage on stems, there's no need to go through the extra labor—although designers' lackeys will complain about having to do your job. But shipped flowers require processing that a local grower's flowers doesn't, so it's just a matter of deciding, along with your client, what the standard is between you—that's a line you'll have to negotiate.

Beating the bees

When someone finds out you grow flowers, inevitably they'll ask if you raise bees. You're going to have to give them the bad news that, while bees are essential for making seed, they're a bane to the cut flower grower.

When a bee pollinates a flower, the flower's business is done. The petals wilt and the private parts put on a new hat, change from attracting a beau to making seed. A flower grower wants his flower to last so anything that makes his blooms race toward seed erodes his product's marketability. If he's growing berries, he needs the bees—without them buds abort and what should have been clusters of berries end up as barren stems—but if he's growing for blooms it's a different story. Snapdragons bloom on a stem from the bottom up, drop their petals as the bees work their way up, too. Delphiniums do the same with the identical result. Some species, like catmint, may get pollinated so quickly that the beautiful blue raceme immediately turns to brown, a less-than-attractive item to provide a designer. Foxglove—bees love it. Asclepias—if you wait a day to allow the bloom to go from one open floret to just a few more, the first florets may have browned, due to pollination, the next day, and the profit margin shrinks.

The bee problem seems more minor in mild climates—the narrow cutting window that opens for many species here gets much wider in cooler climes when less bee pressure exists.

Putting down a bed

As any horse owner knows, there comes a time when it's best to put old Baggins down. The same goes for flower growers: every bed comes to the end of its useful life, so when it reaches the point of being a liability more than an asset you need to pull the plug.

Making the decision regarding annual beds depends on just a couple criteria: when does production wane, when do input costs rise. Some growers mistakenly keep cutting beds long after they should be tilled under, thinking that late blooms equate to blooms with no cost since all the inputs—seeds, planting, fertilizing, irrigating—are already paid. Unfortunately, if weeds invade the bed and approach bud stage or if flower blooms remain unharvested and undeadheaded and threaten to go to seed, the future costs of weeding that area go way up. Add these potential costs to the costs already incurred when you decide to leave a bed intact or to put it down. A weedless bed, a well-deadheaded bed, can remain in production and profitable, but generally the cost of both weeding and deadheading go up as the season progresses, and the cost of NOT weeding and deadheading skyrockets in future years.

Most growers find putting a perennial bed away as painful as putting a pet down. More criteria go into the decision of doing so when compared to an annual bed (getting rid of shrubs can be an even more difficult choice). Quick growing perennials like Heliopsis and Scabiosa, which bloom the first year of planting, require little anguish about eliminating them since they're easily replaced, but the slow growth of Baptisia and expense of Peonies tend to inspire reluctance toward euthanization. Don't hang on to a loved one too long.

Cutting through netting

Inevitably, if you grow flowers you'll end up netting some species, since between the rain and the wind and sometimes vigor alone they may flop and become useless for you as a grower. Nature sometimes intends her creations to flop—a fallen, mature seed head drops its progeny right on the ground, then provides cover to shelter its germination—but you can't really braid crooked stems together and your clients wouldn't want them if you could.

Because netting, like any impediment, makes cutting more difficult, you'll want to weigh the risks of losing a crop against the extra pain of netting and cutting. Anything will flop, given the right conditions—say, a rain storm that makes leaves water-laden, then an immediate wind to push the burdened plant down—but unless you net everything you need to decide how much risk you'll take.

We net most everything in the greenhouses, since without the elements to give the plants a little exercise a single plant falling will make others fall just like the domino theory, but in the field we only net Clematis, Queen Anne's Lace "Green Mist", and snaps—and sometimes, if we're tired or feeling lucky, we don't even net snaps—because these plants flop most of the time. Annual Scabiosa may flop, but if you hold the water back a bit so root zones aren't wet and loose and remain able to hold stems in the wind, you can refrain from netting. Some growers net Delphiniums but we prefer planting extra and taking a certain percentage of loss rather than suffering the added headaches of cutting through net. Generally, taller plants like Dahlias require help, but sturdy species like Amaranth and Sunflowers can withstand storms and wind unless the ground is wet and gives way to the leverage of wind.

You have two choices when cutting through netting, pull the cut stem up or pull the cut stem down, and this will immediately become apparent as you begin cutting, as leaves on the stem will tell you they don't want to leave their positions. Sometimes we cut the netting as we go, as with Bells of Ireland, which won't pull upward because it has multiple stems, but which clings if pulled downward. The cut plastic makes a considerable mess, but because it's so much easier we put up with it. Dusty Miller we treat much the same way.

When you net, start low on the plant to make sure the stems grow through, then raise the netting as the crop heightens to give it support where it requires it. You'll catch on—there should be more stem beneath the net than above, otherwise flopping still can occur.

The best cutters control quality so well in the field that further processing is rarely needed. The fewer mistakes a cutter makes, the better the product, the greater your reputation. The faster the cutter, the more profitable your farm. Recognize the value of the position and treat good help well.

IRRIGATION

⸺◦❧◦⸺

I RRIGATION, IT'S JUST applying water to plants—
how difficult is that?

Quite. It may be the most important and most difficult
of farming's tasks. Unless you only grow crops native to
your climate or are willing to harvest what nature offers
you and not a single stem more, you need to know how
to irrigate.

After decades working on large scale commercial farms
and operating a small cut flower farm, irrigation poses no
mystery to me but I still regularly make mistakes. And it's
all because of the Goldilocks Problem again: too much,
too little, just right. Too much water—kill a succulent or
a species that goes dormant. Too little—kill an aquatic.

You have to know how much water to apply to each
species, but you also need to know your soil type to know
how quickly things dry out, how fast your application
spreads, how far it moves. Sandy soil drains quickly, clay

soil gets soggy easily, loam rests squarely in the middle. And on top of all the water and soil knowledge you need, you have to remember something initially counterintuitive: plants breathe—their roots need air AND water, so too much water means too little air and too little water means too much. This means even clay soil may become too porous if overworked, since rather than having particles closely tied together you may have a layer of clods with large air pockets between them.

Irrigation has no formula, it's not a linear process, though a linear equation's not a bad place to start. It's a lengthy practice you may never wholly complete because each problem you encounter has different variables. You might hope irrigation to be simple, akin to sighting in and shooting a rifle: shoot high, shoot low, find the middle and hit your target. But it's more like shooting a shotgun, where you have a moving target and so go through the same process as with a rifle—high, low, middle—but do it many, many times, until the large number of instances accumulate in your brain and muscles and you become adept at the skill. A popular book claims it takes five thousand hours of practice to excel at any task. If so, prepare for decades before you can gloat about being an irrigation expert.

Irrigation is a matter of moving targets. In most climates the temperature varies, the light-hours change as seasons progress, the wind and subsequent humidity levels range considerably, and all of these factors change the evaporation rate and alter how quickly plants grow (and how they use available water). A proper irrigation in May won't do in August, and mature plants take up a surprising amount of water in the fall even though temperatures drastically lower.

When temperatures turn ninety degrees and above, many plants look to be succumbing to lack of water. Their leaves curl up and droop, and while the plants may in fact be dry, more often you're observing a self-protective mechanism that shrinks the available surface area exposed to the sun so evaporation lessens. You need to check the soil—don't assume it's dry, don't assume it's just the plants protecting themselves, check.

If your acreage possesses many soil types, the drainage varies from place to place, and consequently one section may dry out while another remains quite wet. It wouldn't be unusual to see four or five soil types on the same small acreage, and here, on old acreages where uneven terrain's been scraped and leveled to make gravity irrigation possible, you might see even more. If you grow a hundred species, likely you need to know a hundred rates of water usage, and if you stagger or succession plant those species, you have to adjust to the first planting's need when mature, the second's as it ramps up its growth, and the third's as seedlings. Needless to say, there are a lot of places in the process to make mistakes.

Irrigation is easiest on a very large or very small scale. If you have a million acres of one crop you just have one decision to make, and if you have just one plant you have just one decision to make, but if you have multiple species with different water needs, different lengths of rows requiring different pressures, different types of soil needing varying amounts of water, different plant ages creating a greater range of requirements, then your decisions multiply exponentially. There are a few things to simplify those decision points (which all become possible points of failure, by the way).

Group like with like, species with similar needs together—drought lovers shouldn't be with water-hogs on the same zone, or even in the same row. Even knowing this, there'll be occasions when you have a space that needs filled or a leftover tray of something that leaves you with incompatibles. Just shoot for the middle—water as much as the drought lover can take and still live, and hope you don't water so little that you kill the heavy drinker. It's not a perfect solution, but perfect's not available.

Time and place direct seedings and plantings together. Squeeze your schedule into as few slots as possible so you don't have two rows of Larkspur here and another two there, plus two other sections where you've put Nigella and other early crops. It's just math: if you plant them all at the same time on the same zone you can water them all at once, whereas if you plant in four places in four zones you have four areas to watch.

Give yourself control where possible. We use valves on each line. If you have an acre of Scabiosa and everything gets watered at the same rate, you don't need to valve each line, but if you have ninety species on two acres, sometimes six species on a single row, six different planting dates on six different lines on the same zone, there are going to be differences from line to line so valves give you control. With valves, you can turn off each line as needed. Maybe the delphinium plugs went into the ground earlier in the morning so didn't dry out, and consequently they get enough water before those plugs planted later in the day are sated. Maybe the celosia row needs more water since it's a small seed and needs to stay wet longer, so it needs to stay on. Maybe a part of the field gets more shade and needs less water—the valve lets you turn some lines off while leaving the system on for the rest of the farm.

Most new growers we encounter ask why we don't just run timers, and when they ask we consider their failure rate tripled because technology doesn't answer every problem. They're looking for magic, just like our ancestors, but looking for it in technology, and while apps and timers may assist in certain instances they don't answer any problems completely. Yes, if the entire field consisted of a single crop in a single soil a timer would work, but because species needs vary, planting dates vary, soil types vary you'd need a timer on every line. *You are the timer*!

Being the instrument of control makes you check the progress of your irrigation. You're not exporting your responsibilities to a system, hoping someone else or something else will do your job—why are you farming if you don't want to farm? Go write a computer program.

How do you (how does a timer) know—unless you have years of experience or a very well-oiled set of Tarot Cards—how much water your Heliopsis will need before you begin irrigation? You don't, you can only guess, knowing it's drying out because you see it wilt and after many years you know it's not faking. How do you know it's wet enough and when to stop irrigating? After years of experience, you know that when the surface acquires a chocolate color (color may differ in your area) it's been adequately watered. And still, you leave it on for a couple of hours if the plant is mature, because you know it will take up water fast and you'll just have to irrigate soon if you don't add a little extra. Would a timer do this?

If you do run timers, check the field anyway. If the timer fails, you fail. Checking makes you part of the process, and you can pay attention to other things as you walk the field: insects, weed problems, viral issues.

I could give you a lengthy lesson on flood irrigation, the method used for millennia before electricity came to be (and the method we used for the first five years we were in business). No irrigation method exhibits a lower impact in terms of energy use or carbon footprint, because once a gravity fed canal is built only maintenance remains as an input to keep it moving.

It's an art form with no museum and no awards, though our first landlord may have deserved one. He took immense pride at being able to irrigate his twenty acre truck farm with only a shovel, never having to don a pair of boots. He did this by trickling a stream "no greater than that from a garden hose" down each row, the slow stream preventing erosion and washouts as a stronger stream might. Unfortunately, this meant that the head of the row might soak for forty-eight hours before the stream reached the end a couple hundred feet later when he closed off the flow. Though this made for little waste at the end of the row, a waste other flood farmers often left in the fields as ponds that made the soil salty, it also meant the head end got too much water and the bottom too little.

But he didn't get his shoes wet, it's true.

Fewer and fewer farmers use this method now, though it was how the West was won. Now most farmers use sprinklers, a more efficient way to water if you discount the electricity needed and the infrastructure of pump and aluminum sprinkler lines—and if the farmer refrains from irrigating in the heat of the day when evaporation rates can hit ninety percent.

A more efficient method, in terms of water use at least, arrived with drip irrigation, a low pressure system that trickles small amounts of water through plastic tubing. It requires less electricity, less water, evaporates less, but does use a lot of plastic. And it doesn't take a PhD to put it together, fix it, or use it.

Flood and sprinkler irrigation both put water on the soil surface where it provides sustenance not just for crops but for weeds, too. Flood irrigators face not only the weeds on their own property germinating from surface saturation, but the weed seeds coming down the ditch from neighbors to sweeten the challenge. Sprinkler irrigators who pull from a canal face the problem to a lesser extent, as screens on the sprinkler lines keep larger particles from passing through the flow.

Drip irrigators who place their system above ground deal with surface moisture, too, as anywhere water goes it creates a germination chamber for seeds. But if the drip tape or drip tubing is placed beneath the surface, at root level, water wicks outward, down and up to wet the crop but not any surface seeds (so long as the irrigator shuts the system down before soil becomes saturated). Water use lessens considerably by nearly removing evaporation from the equation.

Drip tape lasts for seven years underground, less above where it gets damaged by sunlight and open air, and we've kept it for ten on the same perennial bed before damage occurs—usually, the weight of the soil and the increased rooting of the plants is the problem, as it eventually chokes the water flow.

Since drip irrigation is a closed system, if you have a clean water source plugging happens but rarely—even underground. Keep screens clean, when you make connections keep fittings clear of dirt and insects (spiders love to nest in open drip valves).

There are many ways to skin a cat and the same goes for plumbing, the field of expertise that drip irrigation is a subset of. When you go to a plumbing store or shop for drip equipment, you may not find what you came for but you can usually find something that works. When you have some spare time, just go to your local plumbing store with a small project in mind, fool with the possible ways to get from point A to point B. It's just like getting from one part of town to another—you may have to take a side route but you'll get there, eventually. You can take a left, a right, and another left, or you can go straight, or take any number of other routes. The way you end up with might not be the most direct way, the fastest way, the best way, or even the easiest way, but it's a way.

There are infinite combinations of configuring drip—barbed ends or threaded (hose thread or pipe), metal or plastic, PVC or poly, compression fittings or clamped (pinch clamps or screw-type), and you can size down from big to little in one step or many, from one type to another—the parts generally come cheap enough that you can even start over rather than continually jerry rigging as we have.

Your problem won't be that you can't do it, your problem will be there are too many ways to do it.

It'd be best, of course, to become an expert at irrigation systems and have all the equations in your head that tell you exactly what you need, but since you're a farmer and you're more interested in plants you probably don't want to become an expert. Still, you need a minimum of knowledge. Keep the Goldilocks problem in mind—if there's too much pressure in your lines you'll blow them out, when there's too little pressure you simply won't be watering evenly. There's some slack between too much and too little, you don't have to be perfect—that's the beauty of the system, it's uncomplicated. The perfect pressure is when the drip tape has the feel of a slightly underinflated bicycle tire.

Too little pressure has less system repercussion because you can't damage anything, and most growers bypass the too much pressure problem by running pressure regulators that check the flow. Since our system has a gazillion zones and we'd need fifty or sixty regulators, we take a different tack by designing branch lines with tubing size that limits the maximum pressure. Any particular size of tubing can only accept so much water pressure before friction kicks in with all its might, so in a tubing properly sized down the pressure cannot exceed what drip tape can withstand.

We size down our mainline from inch and a quarter at the head to one for branch lines and then one step further, to three quarters, as we tee off toward each zone (a set of T-tape lines). Your zone sizes depend on your tape purchase, and your supplier has a table of just how many gallons per hour per foot that style of tape emits—it differs between low flow and high, between four inch spacing, eight inch and twelve. Your supplier can help you, just hold your frustrations back. If worst comes to worst, just give it the trial and error method, making sure you start at the "not enough" pressure side of the problem, then working your way up to where you want to be.

The task of running a system without regulators becomes a problem on small zones where water demand is low but water pressure is high—our greenhouses irrigate from a high pressure well, and though there can be as many as a hundred 100 foot lines the scheduling of multiple crops with multiple needs and multiple planting times means that rarely does everything need water simultaneously. For partial irrigations, we "feather" the hydrant handle open, check for flow, feather it further open, check again—until we have the right amount of water in the lines. It's a dangerous method as it's easy to blow out drip tape when pressure runs at double its maximum threshold.

If you're a small farmer, times arise when a specific

area needs water but the rest of the farm doesn't. The pump needs to be on to irrigate, but the pump has only on and off and can't be feathered like a hydrant handle. Pumps, like cars, run best when used within certain parameters, but they will operate outside them—just not without doing eventual damage. Low pressure can burn a pump out immediately—if it doesn't have back pressure and starts pushing and pulling air, it won't last long—and high pressure makes it work harder, putting stress on all components that over time has negative effects. So in order to run your system inside the parameters it best operates, designate a slack area, a place you can irrigate where extra water won't hurt so you can turn the pump on without damaging it and still water the small area that needs a drink. We just open zones to our windbreaks since trees and shrubs are more forgiving when overwatered than are annuals and some perennials.

Just as checking and rechecking your system is essential to make sure no failures exist, you need to check and recheck your soil to assess when a crop needs water. Dig into the ground, grab a handful of soil, compress it. If, when you let go, it neither crumbles nor feels sticky, it's perfect—which means it needs water soon if the weather is hot and it's a mature plant, or it doesn't if the weather's cool and it's a young plant.

Irrigating just-planted seedlings requires a different strategy. Since they dry out quickly we soak plugs immediately before planting, then start the irrigation system up and soak them as soon as we plant—and then soak them again two or three days later, after checking them a couple times a day to make sure they remain moist.

Transplants need constant attention during the transition period from greenhouse to field, since the soil they've been planted in doesn't interface perfectly with their new home—the particles of the two medium don't match, so air pockets remain and it takes time for the two to bond (after all, it's an arranged marriage). The soil's been broken, much as you might cut your finger, so it takes some time to heal. If it rains you're in luck, because the weight of the water above seals the cut better than water coming from below. Once the cut has healed, irrigation becomes easier because the "crumb" of the soil is more predictable.

The key here, both in terms of soil and irrigation system: CHECK! Check your work, check the lines, check to see if you actually turned on each line, check the end of the lines to make sure water has reached (if you've run over an area with the tractor, the tape may have been compressed, a valve may have failed and plugged—if water's reached the end, the line's working), check the head end to make sure no lines have been knocked off by laborers or excess pressure, check the screens and clean as necessary.

And then a couple hours later, check again. As a row darkens to chocolate from additional moisture you know it nears saturation, and expect the moisture to continue wicking after you turn it off. A row that seems a little dry at the end of the day may turn out to be perfectly saturated in the morning—with practice you'll learn the wicking rate. A good farmer knows his farm, and knows it by monitoring the progress of the irrigation, the presence of insect or weed intruders. You never reach a point when because you have experience the farm will take care of itself, you just get better at monitoring. If it was easy, everyone would do it.

Other Notes:

Drip irrigation won't push up hill because it runs at such low pressure, but if you have a slope, as we do, just run a mainline to the high end and run the driplines the other way, downslope.

When creating or altering your system, understand that any impediment lessens pressure—connectors, screens, injectors, tees—so don't install them on the system further upstream than necessary.

If you pull water from a dirty source, either buy an expensive screen that does the job all at once or use inexpensive screens that split the job, a large mesh (i.e., 32) early in the system to screen out the big chunks, then smaller as you move down the line. Though drip line ideally runs water through 200 mesh filters, so much sediment comes in our water that a 200 fills and plugs many times a day, so we do with 100s and have little problem.

If you have strong winds, water tall plants like sunflowers sparingly so the root zone doesn't saturate and loosen, allowing plants to topple. Water early in the day, before winds come up (unless your wind patterns differ), and not so much that the plants can't take up much of the moisture before it gets windy. Earlier in their lives, sunflowers can be soaked without problem, but when taller the torque of a thirty mile wind on a six foot high stem with a head that acts like a wind sock is great enough to knock a sunflower over.

Turn the water off on species like Eremerus or Allium when they go dormant. In fact, many bulb crops don't really want more than a minuscule amount of water once they quit making leaves, as they just require enough to keep root growth going and prevent desiccation. Try to group dormant crops together so you can forget about them later in the year (but still check the property for weeds).

Check connections for tightness when you make them, then check them again when you operate them. It's easier to put them together when they're warm, so in cold weather have a small butane burner handy to soften tubing. This makes it pliable for tees, connectors, elbows and especially compression fittings. Don't use the burner for the T-tape, though, or you will melt it. Make cuts clean and at 90 degrees, as slanted or rough cuts tend to leak.

The Goldilocks Problem illustrates itself most vividly in irrigation. If you "bank" water by irrigating plants heavily, you also make an ideal environment for weed seed to germinate, and if you water exactly how much a plant needs, you'll need to water more often as it takes that water up. It's your choice: water more frequently and weed less, water less frequently and more heavily and weed more. You might find the sweet spot, where you can bank a bit of water without weeding too much more—who knows, you might get lucky!

PART TWO

TIPS FOR GROWERS

Tip #1. One of the problems of being a new grower—or new anything—is the small sample size that early experience comprises. It's easy to connect things that happen that aren't really connected in a cause and effect way until you've seen enough events to figure out that they might be simultaneous or synchronous but unrelated. If you throw a dice and it comes up a six five or six times in a row, you may think you will always roll a six if you're rationalizing badly. But if you roll the dice a hundred times you'll realize you're wrong, because events even out with a big sample size and you'll start getting the other numbers on the dice. New growers often believe a technique they used worked just because the events coincided—they sprayed milk and fungus went away, planted two crops together and had no insect pressure that year. There may be a connection, but until they repeat the procedure many times under different conditions, they can't really say one event caused the other. If you make that kind of spurious logic many times, you'll fail. Keep a "maybe it works" in the back of your mind, then try to disprove or prove your assumption. Otherwise you can find yourself in a logical cul-de-sac—and it might prove costly.

Tip #2. Adding steps doesn't make things easier, necessarily. Taking away steps usually does. Don't be fooled by gimmicks, techniques, magic formulas or potions or equipment—you can't add to subtract. If one thing takes two things out of a process, check it out, but otherwise be skeptical. Most new things aren't better things—if you don't believe me, watch the commercials on late afternoon TV.

Tip #3. Pests aren't naturally drawn to unhealthy plants—a plague of locusts doesn't leave healthy plants and devour only sickly ones. There is some evidence that plants can chemically repel insects to a degree, but not to the degree required for the appearance-oriented cut flower industry. If you've paid attention to a single outbreak of aphids or spider mites, you'll know that they spread from one plant to its neighbors and don't take inventory as doctors might, deciding to only take the weak and infirm first. This idea might be derived from biologists seeing that predators take the weak and elderly first—but the category for predators is "easy" and "difficult", so they take the slowest first just as you, if you're hungry, might stop at the gas station for a burrito, even though you know it's lousy food and you'd rather be eating Pad Thai at a good restaurant. If you don't believe me, take a wolf to a butcher shop and see if he refuses the good cuts of meat.

Tip #4: There are no magic potions. Euphorbia may deter a gopher that meets its less than tasty root, but gophers can travel above ground and won't necessarily be deterred. Deer don't eat daffodils, but even a field of daffodils won't prevent the deer from walking from one place to another to find other tasty things among them.

Tip #5. Scale. Washing aphids off plants may work in the garden, but at some point a plot of land becomes too large for small scale solutions. Understand the limitations of your techniques in regards to the scale of your operation—a big tractor won't fit in a greenhouse, a tiller won't work five acres, and it's pretty hard to drag a hose around four or five acres in order to wash aphids off infested plants. Be prepared to change your view of what works and what doesn't as you move from one size of operation to another.

Tip #6. If you live in a snowy area and want to get ahead of the game, apply a dark substance on the snow—graphite, compost, ash—to absorb sunlight and heat. Opening up the "seal" of winter even a bit exacerbates the melt exponentially, that's why a small open area on the Earth's poles quickly expands (research "albedo" for a fascinating read). Area dry farmers occasionally fly graphite onto their fields to speed up the melt and prevent winter wheat beneath from dying or getting fungal outbreaks. It doesn't take much material to really ramp up the melt—a vegetable farmer near here in zone 3 had eating peas ready the first week of June by spreading compost on the three-foot high snow where his pea row would be.

Tip #7. The balance of nature isn't your balance or my balance, and certainly isn't a balance favoring the perfectionist demands of cut flower buyers. It includes population explosions, wild climate fluctuations, cataclysms and extinctions, a much wider perspective than our own ideas of "harmony". Since we occasionally use chemicals to combat insects, we often get a condescending nod from organic farmers who know our problem comes from destroying the ecosystem's "balance". I'm inclined to think that insect problems are more complicated, more area- and weather-based. If a fellow flower farmer who grows organically two hundred miles away, in identical soil with similar temperatures but in a warmer zone, has aphids in his viburnum I will invariably have them a month later at a similar stage of growth, and if he doesn't, I won't have to worry about mine. Pest infestations can be very widespread and all-encompassing, despite one's methods of dealing with them. Another example: Asclepias species get regularly infested with aphids in his area, while in ours aphids attack about one in ten years. Does he get aphids because he farms organically and tries to keep a balanced ecosystem? I doubt it. It's more likely that a subset of aphids has taken a liking over the years to Asclepias in his immediate area, or perhaps a neighboring farm harbors a "mother" species that spreads its young downwind to him. Don't make connections that don't exist—believe what you will, but believe facts first. If there's a balance of nature, it's not a fixed and static thing, and if you blame your insect problems on your failure to maintain a "balance" you're in for a long career of self-flagellation.

Tip #8. Seize the day—take opportunities when they arise. The nearby town of Blackfoot, like many small cities across the US, is bisected by railroad tracks, and there are only four opportunities to get from one side of town to the other. If you're driving down Main and see the first crossing open, you have a hundred percent chance of getting to your destination without delay. It may not be the street you want to be on, but it's easy enough to get to where you want to be once you're across the track. If you wait for the exact street you want to drive down, you may find a train in your way and a forty-five minute wait that makes you late for school or work. Taking opportunities is a game of percentages—if you wait to get the best price for something you want to buy, you risk not only not getting it at all but lose all the time spent searching for it; if you demand the highest price for your goods, you may risk not selling them at all; if you wait for the perfect time to till, to plant, to harvest, you may face weather that sets you back so far you lose your opportunity completely. And on top of all that, what does it do for your psyche— the niggling needed to hit the perfect price or moment erodes character, overrides the benefits of that adrenaline rush that comes from rolling the dice and being perfect and right.

Tip #9. Check your work. Check others' work. Check the things that are supposed to do your checking, like timers. Then check it all again. Thermostats and timers can fail. You may have a drip line you forgot to open. The propane tank may be empty. A wind may have loosened the greenhouse wiggle wire. You may have left a cooler door open. Anything can happen at anytime, be aware of your farm and infrastructure. Anyone can have a "toaster moment", that instant when you remember you left the toaster on, usually coming when you're an hour down the road on a trip to the airport, so check yourself (without becoming obsessive, of course).

Tip #10. Don't save money. Well, save it, but don't think that's the important thing about your business—making money, not saving money, is. So what if a plant costs a dollar if you make two—it's better than getting a free plant and making fifty cents. The math you should be doing is profit minus cost, not "how little did I spend" or "how much did I save". Many new growers come from household budgets, which are fixed, so they're thinking about saving money, but a business income isn't fixed, it's open-ended. The "save" mindset has to change for a business to succeed. That means it may make more sense to pay somebody else to do something you can do yourself. It means you can spend money to make money, that spending money isn't necessarily a negative thing in your bank account. It means you may be better off buying new things rather than used, which, while generally cheaper, can cost more if they need to be upgraded or fixed, particularly if you lack the skills to maintain them. It means realizing that free things usually aren't free—foraging sounds like a no-brainer, but unless you live next door to a source you still have to drive, it still takes your time to find and process product, so you need to understand there is a cost. It means rethinking waste, because while it may be anathema to you, it might be more profitable than saving. For instance, if it costs time and money to keep plants like tulips and ranunculus for extra seasons then buying new ones may actually be more profitable. You have to store, maintain beds, weed, and irrigate free, multi-year bulbs and corms, so keep those costs in mind when you consider holding on to old plant material. And, if you lose a cropping period in a hoophouse or greenhouse because you're holding on to a non-producing crop, add that to the deficit side of your bank account. If you dig up dahlias, allium, gladiolas, total the hours you put in digging them, the time storing them and the risk of losing them if you store them improperly, and measure that against the cost of replacements.

Removing "saving" from the foremost of your decision making, you need to remember when buying something of great cost to consider its re-sale value: if you decide to sell it, your cost will be the difference between what you paid and what you make from the sale—not, as the savings mentality would scarily have it, the initial cost only. Land, tractors and equipment, coolers, these are easily marketed items; greenhouses, less so. Pay good help. Paying a bad employee minimum wage doesn't save money, paying a good one who does triple the work makes you money—why wouldn't you pay him or her triple the wages if that much more work is done? Be generous—stinginess rubs off on those around you, including your clients. You want to be paid fairly so why wouldn't you want to pay others fairly, too? If you're thinking about saving, you're huddling, hoarding, acting like you're under siege; if you're thinking about making money, you're open to possibility, you have your eyes open, ready to meet opportunity.

Tip #11. Avoid even the appearance of amateurishness. Dress properly. That doesn't mean suit and tie or evening gown and four-inch heels, nor does it mean so casual that you look slovenly. Don't do as I did in our early days, go to your clients straight out of the field, in muddy boots, patched pants, bedraggled with a sweaty hat. First appearances are important—eventually, quaint and farmerly might win you points, but initially clients will be taken aback. Your delivery vehicle should be full, abundant, because no one buys from sparseness—don't you just go right back out the door if you see shelves mostly bare, do you take the last piece of pizza? We've seen new growers show up with three stems of this and four of that—it makes you look like you don't know what you are doing. And keep like with like, don't mix up your flowers, make them easy to see and differentiate. Clients want to know how much is available, and how big your bunches are, so you have to sleeve them unless you have pre-orders.

Don't expect wholesalers to greet you with open arms. They have dozens, often hundreds of clients and they can't afford to bring you on board until they are sure of your product and your ability to provide it. We faxed a wholesaler weekly for three years before he showed up at our field and realized we were serious growers (luckily, we had half an acre—way too much—of larkspur just starting to bloom, and our fields were weed-free). You are the one asking for something, the onus of proving yourself is on you—wholesalers can't take chances, they have to be sure you can produce and be professional. You are not owed a place in their stable just because you are you.

Have relatively uniform product. It doesn't have to be stem to stem exact—we have clients who appreciate our sunflowers being cut in different stages, because that makes an arrangement seem alive, in process, rather than static and finished—but it can't be a combination of one foot stems and three foot stems.

Don't have dirty buckets—nothing turns off a client like the smell of two week old water, even if they do love kambucha.

Remember, selling is a lot like dating. It's a relationship. Look good at first to get attention, keep looking good to get respect. And if you weren't or aren't good at dating, you will be after doing the flower farming gig.

Tip #12. Don't rely on common sense—it's not only uncommon but can be totally wrong. Your mind often performs prejudicial calculations without looking at the big picture. For instance, it seems like one degree warmer in a greenhouse wouldn't be that big of a deal, right? But raising the temperature of a 2000 square foot greenhouse with double poly plastic from 35 degrees to just 36 takes 10% more BTU's when the outside temperature is 25.

Another instance of a "small" thing being a "big" one (and you know this one): leave one weed to go to seed and there may be 50,000 next year.

Here's another one that strikes acquaintances as common sense: if WalMart sells a lot of Poinsettias or Easter Lilies, I should be able to, too. Big picture: Box stores sell a lot of things, like holiday centered plants, for less than cost so you come to the store to buy something with a bigger markup. I'd be a fool to compete with that marketing scheme.

Yet another example: It seems dumb to friends that we turn down any sale, but if a customer comes to our farm and takes a half hour of our time to buy a ten dollar (or even a fifty dollar) bouquet, we've lost money—it's more sensible to turn down such interactions.

Check your initial prejudices, expand your attention from the "obvious" to include a wider look at whatever you do and you might find a more accurate viewpoint.

Tip #13. Hit 'em where they ain't. If you want to get into a new market, you can either copy what's already being done and force your way into it or look for openings that allow you to just waltz right in with no trouble at all. In our nearby town, most new businesses try the copy method—if someone opens a semi-successful pizza joint, there'll be four more just like it within a year and then they'll all be broke soon after. If you're just copying what others do, you either have to do it better or more cheaply to succeed, but if you do something new you're at the forefront (and of course, if you're successful others will start copying you). So if no one's selling succulents, sell succulents. If you're a designer develop a different style than other designers. Provide tables, chairs, linens, tents for events, take that load off your clients' plate. Invent events. Grow something different by manipulating your climate, tweaking the seasons so your product comes on at a different time—an open space in the market. If you're in a place where "everything's been done", your open area is going to have to be service. That means giving up some of your comfort to ease your clients' worries and stresses—only you can decide whether it's worth it. In mature markets there aren't many open spaces, it's true, but in the floral trade right now there's yet room to grow.

Tip #14. The Goldilocks Problem. It's everywhere you turn on a flower farm. The seeds are too big, too little, just right for the seeder plates. The soil's too wet, too dry, just right to work. The flower's too open, too closed, just right to harvest. The transplants are too far apart, too close, just right. If your mind tends toward the need for right and wrong, black and white, you'd best either retrain yourself or find another enterprise, because the "just right" on the farm shifts from person to person, moment to moment— that's how quality, as opposed to quantity, operates, as a spectrum rather than an either/or equation.

If the crop's not quite just right and you have an order for it, you may shift "just right" and cut it a tad more closed than you normally would. If it's going to rain and you need to till and the soil's not quite where "just right" normally is, well, you have to shift your standards and work it when it's a little too wet. If you don't, maybe those transplants will sit in their cells too long and they'll be ruined.

When you irrigate and have crops with different needs on the same row or zone, you can't have "just right" for all of them. You have to short the water-hungry, slightly drown the drought-tolerant, aim for the middle, a new "just right".

Your employee's going to think "just right" is different than you do—he puts more water or less in the buckets than you think you told him to; his six-inch spacing is closer or further apart than yours (or so you think until you see that your spacing wavers as the day progresses, too); the tautness of the netting he puts up is looser than you want, or maybe it's too tight, or maybe your assessment today differs from what it was yesterday. You're going to need to be flexible, extend your standards from "exactly this" to "within this range."

You're going to order too many plants or too few, have too much room or too little—it's inevitable, accept it. The plug producer will send you plants too developed (rootbound) or underdeveloped (dirt falling off, exposing the roots)—your responding tantrum won't help.

In terms of color, your "lavender", your "peach", your "salmon", won't be everyone else's. Color comes in a spectrum, and people slice it up in different ways. You're not right, they're not right, but you need to determine what they mean and match it to what you mean. A more orange red, a more blue lavender, a more pastel yellow— some of us (me, for instance) will take years to determine the shades, others (like Jeriann, who, as an artist, has been dealing with color for decades) can spot differences from a hundred yards and identify the exact accepted names for them (though clients and employees names rarely match hers, she can shift her understanding to include theirs). Caerulean blue, quinachrodome rose, new gamboge, aurolian yellow—these are very accurate names to watercolorists who share understanding, but even longtime designers may not recognize them, instead having their own, less accurate nomenclature. But the differences in shade make a great deal of difference to a bride so you must pay attention to them. Color is a quality, not a quantity.

The list of Goldilocks problems runs on and on, as you can see, and you no doubt already have encountered it a considerable number of times. But if you stop and think about how unreasonable exactitude is in regards to what farming's all about, you'll probably start cutting yourself and others a little slack—and maybe even experience a little humor or irony as you do.

Tip #15. If someone or something makes your pixie dust bell ring, best cock your pistol, hold up your cross, or murmur a protective hex. It's entirely possible something that sounds perfect and wonderful really is just that, but it's also highly improbable.

There's always been a lot of dream-selling going on in every time period, but it seems more prevalent than ever since the Internet allows everyone access to everyone else. Magical lifestyles, farming techniques that will change the world, instant success—the people selling these things are sometimes so steeped in belief that they're really not aware of any downside to their offerings, but some are well aware of the human need for magic and are capitalizing on it. That doesn't make them evil—though whoever is selling that red, white and blue rose seed does make the evil list in my mind—but you do need to be aware that what they sell may work for them not because it actually worked for them, but because *you're buying the idea that it did and does.*

At present in the flower farming business a great many people are selling the ideas of flower farming as a lifestyle and techniques to farm flowers that are "easy" and magical, not to mention selling their reputation as designers to those hoping to ride their success train. For us, flower farming has been magical, just not in the way it's being sold and understood. And it can be easy, but not easy in the way that it is sold. And it can be a fantastic lifestyle, but again, not as sold. It's like when you buy an electronic toy or other item, then get home to see that 'batteries aren't included"—READ THE FINE PRINT!

So investigate the claims being made. Does the purveyor make (or has he ever made) a living from what he promotes—a living as good as the one you want—or does he make his living from promoting? Does the technique fit your acreage size, your soil type, your climate, or is it specific to his? Is the technique so sophisticated that it requires many years to duplicate—are you being taught basketball by LeBron James, art by Picasso, cello by Yo-Yo-Ma, when you're just a beginner? Most of all, are you just taken in because his ideology fits yours, when neither yours nor his has actually been tested in the real world?

There's no more important lesson to learn than this one, and I have yet to completely learn it even at my advanced age—I bought a windmill during the wind-craze a few years back, and now I basically have an eight thousand dollar lawn ornament (better than a gnome, I suppose). It's easy to be caught not just by carnival barkers and hucksters but by politicians and the well-meaning, so while it's never good to be crass and cynical it's always helpful to be at least a little bit skeptical.

Tip #16. Fall planting. Few things work as fall plantings in our zone 5 high desert climate. Only Bupleurum, Larkspur, and Nigella come to mind, with the latter being no better than a "maybe". Generally speaking, fall plantings face two major problems through the winter: if they get too large their surface area is exposed to cold winds and temperatures so they succumb, and if they're too small they're not strong enough to make it through winter unless there's snow cover. Snow cover is an essential factor for cold weather growers—we can depend on snow on a regular basis but not snow cover, since winds bare the soil in most places and deposit it deeply in others. Both bare and deep present a problem, as no snow cover means more openness to cold and wind, and too much cover presents the possibility of soggy soil and consequently frozen roots. We don't even try to plant fall plugs anymore, since they generally lack the warmth and time to root properly for a hard winter. So experiment until you're satisfied you know what works in your area, but don't assume it's either possible or impossible just because you read of another's success (or failure).

Tip #17. Complete tasks—figuratively, not literally. Doing a task isn't necessarily completing it. You've probably told a child to alert a sibling that dinner was ready, and the child stood right beside you and yelled "dinner's ready!"—don't be that child. And don't be the guy who signals a turn just feet before the intersection, rather than distant enough to let you know you could continue on your way. Signaling isn't to prove you did something, it's to alert other drivers of your intention.

Every bit of speech is just a verbal map—a piece of information compressing a larger chunk of information in order to make reality more negotiable. If I have to make a more accurate map, have to say "Tell your sister dinner's ready by going downstairs, looking her in the eye, speaking, making sure she understands," then you're making my life—and consequently yours—more difficult. As a child or an employee, you may have deflected responsibility using this ploy, but as a farmer and business owner, it's just not going to work. You will suffer the consequence of not fully embracing the meaning of the task.

You may turn the water on, but did you check the lines to make sure they weren't clogged, that they were lying between the rows, that no breaks were evident?

You may put the transplants in, but did you actually bury them beneath the soil level or did you just go through the motions of sticking them in?

You may walk the transplants after you're done to look for mistakes, but did you actually look or were you bored and miss the exact thing you were supposed to be looking for?

When you weed, do you just walk the rows? That isn't weeding.

When you email a client or put out an Instagram, do you make sure the message was received? If not, you didn't do anything at all except make yourself feel like you did something—just like a child yelling "dinner's ready!"

Tasks have an aim, an intent, and you can pretend to do them, emulate doing them, even convince yourself you've done them when you haven't completed them at all. As a child, you might get away with it; as a driver, you'll probably just irritate others; as an employee, your boss might let you slide just because he's weary. But as the farmer, the owner, the businessman, you pay for your hollow effort. When you catch yourself pretending, when you hear yourself making an excuse, correct yourself and improve your chance at success.

Tip #18. Units. For lack of a better term (I'm sure somewhere out there in academia there's a proper term for what I'll be discussing). The atoms of flower farming, the unbreakable parts that can't be torn down further. Just like you can't have the average American family of 2.2 children, but can have 2 kids or 3 kids and nothing in between, coolers don't come in parts, nor do greenhouses, acreages, rows—the list is endless. Simple as that sounds, it may be one of the most important concepts in terms of profitability, because you need to maximize your units' usage. Let me explain.

Your vehicle is a complete, unbreakable unit. You have to buy the same amount of gas whether it's full of flowers or has two bunches in it: your profit goes down as its contents shrink in amount. Fill it when possible.

Your greenhouse is a complete, unbreakable unit. It costs the same to heat a full one as a half-full one. Plant it all and your costs shrink since they're spread out over the entire planting. Plant quick-turning plants, add to your profit. Don't waste all that heated airspace on seeds—find a smaller unit to grow those in.

A row is complete. Fill it. Empty spots will still be watered and weeded—perhaps weeded more because it's open.

A trip to one client just as well turn into a trip to many (unless you have a very sizeable order). Shrink your costs by spreading them over many clients. Your trip is a unit, its costs fixed but its profits malleable.

A box is a unit, whether it's empty or full, and it costs the same to ship either way, so fill it up if you're sending out, order complete boxes of plants and such if you're ordering in, to shrink your costs.

A cooler is a single unit, its costs basically the same whether full or empty. Maximize its usage, if possible.

Scale is all about units. If your unit to be serviced is your farmstand, three dahlias of one kind, four snapdragon plants, ten sunflowers might be enough to fill it with mixed bouquets, but if your unit of service is a client(s) you need to adjust your plantings to her (their) needs—three dahlias won't service even one event for one client, and it certainly won't do a wholesaler any good. Your client base is a unit—the more completely you service it, the less you waste.

It's a simple idea, the unbreakable unit, sometimes a complex, unsolvable problem, and you'll encounter it often. The better you manage it in terms of efficiency, the more profitable you'll be.

Tip #19. Working with others. There's a Buddhist parable about two monks, one blind and strong as an ox, the other frail and old but having perfect vision. They solved the problems of how to get around by having the blind man carry the weak but sighted one and thus they were able to negotiate their way through the world—seeing with the weak man's eyes, moving with the blind man's strength. Working with your significant other might be much the same—so long as you know your weaknesses and your strengths and use them in unison.

Be prepared for the split personality of flower farming—marketing and growing are two different skill sets, and few of us have both (though perhaps we're all capable of acquiring them). If you're lucky you have a spouse that provides one role while you perform the other, and if you're even luckier you both know the boundaries of your responsibilities—who's boss where and when. But even then, there'll be problems.

Problems occur at the interface of boundaries. If you've built a house, you know that the electrician has to deal with the drywaller who has to deal with the plumber who has to deal with the tile guy—they have different disciplines, but there are places where they meet, where you have to arbitrate who does what and in what order they do it.

Likewise, look at a map. Some national boundaries, like mountain ranges and rivers, are obvious, but many are arbitrarily drawn lines where most troubles occur. Just look at the national boundaries in the Middle East or Africa, see the lack of natural boundaries between Russia and Europe, and you'll understand history better. Take a page from history to establish clear ways to negotiate where those arbitrary lines meet in *your* life and on *your* farm or you'll have some World Wars, too. The key is identifying the borders, then lowering the level of erosion and explosion where two separate entities meet.

The boundary between growing and marketing is about as clear a line as you'll find in flower farming. A grower has to get things done, he might start out thinking of perfect ways but a half an hour into his day the whole framework's shot. He's like a juggler using live animals instead of bowling pins. Nature moves, conditions change, he's in a constant dialogue with moving targets and has to adjust and know he's likely to fail—hopefully, in small, non-lethal increments.

A marketer, on the other hand, while still a juggler, has to be a perfectionist. She cannot make mistakes. She's juggling time-bombs, deadlines and orders made by fretful designers and more fretful clients, pressure heightened by the perishable nature of the product being sold. The marketer has to have people skills, can't be rushed, needs aplomb, has to listen, has to pay attention to detail, has to present a professional demeanor at all times.

When we started Bindweed Farm, we were small enough for me to do both tasks (badly). I quickly found that I was thinking of farm needs while I marketed and thinking of marketing needs while I farmed. Consequently, I always felt panicky, in a hurry and unfocussed on the task at hand. It wasn't until Jeriann jumped on board with the aesthetic and people end of the farm process that the business started thriving. I could concentrate on growing, she could attend to marketing—we worked together, but in separate arenas.

Good fences make good neighbors because they establish clear boundaries: there's here and there, this side and that side; there's still the fence itself, another story that can wait. You have to be clear about whose domain is whose. Don't be alphabetizing her spice rack if she's the cook, and don't rearrange his tools if he's the mechanic. Nonetheless, he may have to cook from time to time when she's not around, and she may need to fix something if he's not available. Have a process to deal with those times—don't get overly rigid about this, have some SLACK: wiggle room for differences, the place of tolerances so the invader doesn't have to be perfect.

Because Jeriann handles clients and money coming in, she does the books for accounts receivable. She has a system that I might be able to figure out with a minimal amount of effort, but there's no reason to get involved with her work unless for some reason it's not getting done (it always gets done). I do accounts payable, because I do all the running for parts, the plant ordering, the myriad little expenses that make up any business, so it makes no sense for her to do the books for those things: she'd have to be asking me questions about categories, amounts, etc… which would make the total time for the task longer than me doing it. Efficiency needs to define the rule-making about these things: make a program, a process, that simplifies, streamlines, takes less time and effort, creates less stress and strain.

Don't be passive-aggressive. That means don't say the other has authority, then undermine it by making comments or decisions not up to you. You can suggest markets for her to enter, but it's her decision whether or not to work them—since she has to do the work and has all the risk, it's her call. And you have to be fine with that—no grumbling, no resentment, just turn away and grow. She can suggest plants to grow, but it's your decision whether or not to grow them. After all, you have to amend the soil for their needs, irrigate them, and harvest them. If they're difficult, you won't want to do it.

Be diligent. If you're the mechanic and she needs something fixed, fix it. If you don't, don't be upset when she gets someone else to do it. And if you're supposed to box up an order, do it. Don't be upset if he does it because you forgot it in the thick of things. Have SLACK. Be tolerant.

There can be intertwining action between you, but there can't be constant negotiation—someone has to be the boss. If you want to see what happens with many bosses, watch Congress, and if you want to see what happens with a single boss, check out how quickly things move in China. Negotiation slows things down for mathematical reasons: one thing travels faster than two or many. But a farm has too much going on for one boss—split it into arenas of action, have dictators in each arena that meet from time to time in a democratic, egalitarian fashion.

Tip #20. Infrastructure. I didn't learn much working on a conventional farm for fifteen years, but I did learn that a lot of farmers went broke by spending too much on every new thing and piece of infrastructure. But I also learned that a lot of them went broke by not keeping up with the times, by spending too little, having broken down equipment, not fitting in with the trends that were leaving them behind. There's a fine line between too much and too little spending—the Goldilocks problem again.

I've been a sucker for gadgets since I saw x-ray specs for sale on the inside cover of comic books, but I recognize that enthusiasm now and squash it immediately. There's an equation you need in your head when it comes to whether to incorporate technology into your operation, and it differs from farm to farm, farmer to farmer. For us, if it means more labor, it's a no, if it means less, it's a maybe.

We don't like techniques you need to repeat, like lifting off row cover. For us, the nightly battle with wind to cover rows coupled with the morning battle of rolling cover up is just too much to bear. We already have too much on our plate, so we let the frost do what it will, even though we know that covers extend our growing season. We've never figured it out on paper whether buying cover, hoops, and costing out labor makes up for the added revenue, but it's my hunch that as costs go up, profits go down.

Permanent structures strike a different note for us—you can pay for a greenhouse in a year or two and once it's up, and maintenance is pretty low. There aren't any hours spent covering and uncovering, replacing torn materials, just harvesting and planting and a little weeding, three costs that never go away no matter what. And it's there for decades, with only the plastic to replace every four or five years.

I'm not a tool guy, so it makes my decisions easier than they would be for someone who loves to fiddle with fixing. It's easy for me to say no since I can't use a tool, anyway, but I do have a couple rules to follow: single-use tools are money-suckers, for the most part. We have a posthole digger we bought to make holes for our greenhouses, but it's been sitting idle for a decade—wouldn't it have been better to rent one? I bought a chipper—and gave it away, I needed it so rarely. I thought I wanted a mechanical transplanter, but thought better of buying it when I admitted that it wasn't that difficult to plant fifteen thousand plugs, especially when soil conditions would dictate frequently adjusting the transplanter.

In general, avoid any piece of technology that can't be easily fixed or replaced, or if broken shuts down an entire process. And remember that, while complex technology can sometimes simplify tasks, you still need to pay attention and make sure it's working—just revisit Three Mile Island to see how secondary and tertiary systems, assumed to work, created the problem.

A cart to move buckets around might be nice, but for me, a little extra hand labor saves a trip to the gym.

And adding steps to a process drives me nuts—why get the perfect tool, do it the perfect way, when I can do it imperfectly much more quickly and just be done. It's easy to get in the habit of making things easy, and the mindset of backing off from work can quickly turn into a way of avoiding getting things done. For me it's a matter of bulling my way through work to I can veg out with a novel and a cup of coffee, while those of you who want a gentler way of working may make your decisions based on your lifestyle choice. There's no fixed rule, unless you're only considering monetary gains—only then does it become obvious what choices you should make.

Tip #21. When Jeriann taught junior high students and younger for fifteen years, she often encountered talented students "too smart to learn." The naturally gifted art students, having so dazzled their family and peers for their entire lives, refused to listen to her instruction—maybe they thought she was old, or that she wouldn't know anything, despite her decades of learning to draw and paint under other masterful instructors. Just a few tiny tips, if incorporated, might have taken these students down a path toward artistic success, but years later they still painted and drew just as they had as junior high students. They'd never grown.

So, give yourself a good think: are you as smart as you think you are, or too smart for your own good? If you've read lots of books about farming, if you've gone to lots of conferences, googled every plant and method—you may be *too* smart. If you have too many things in your head, you can't really see and you can't really listen, so when a problem comes up, rather than dealing with it directly you draw upon your knowledge and it may get in the way.

Philosophers make a distinction between "knowing that" and "knowing how". You can know everything about building bicycles, riding bicycles, the laws of physics governing the possibility of bicycling, but until you ride a bicycle you don't know how to; your knowledge may impede you so much that you don't learn as quickly as someone who's ignorant, someone who takes every bicycle fall as feedback to change his behavior.

So don't let your preconceptions get in the way. Learn to know how rather than know that.

Tip #22. Accept Facts. Don't try to reconcile the irreconcilable. Early in my farm career an informal mentor in the ASCFG helped me with setting up my drip irrigation system. I mentioned I was having a hard time cultivating without running over the valves and asked him what I should do. "Don't run over them," he replied.

Doh! It was an AHA moment for me. I realized that many of my questions had their solutions in my posing of them—that there were no answers, that I was just throwing the adult version of a childish tantrum: I want the problem to stop, Mommy!

Some problems don't have solutions other than the obvious ones. Some actions just have consequences and you accept them or do things differently. That's what growing up and becoming an adult is all about, and that's what farming should do to you: make you an adult. If you don't become one, well, you'll fail.

Q. Alcoholic: How do I stop drinking?
A. Stop drinking.
Q. Smoker: How do I stop smoking?
A. Stop smoking.
Q. Dieter: How do I eat less?
A. Eat less.

Entire industries thrive from making simple things complicated, by taking advantage of our impulse to have something outside ourselves solve something within. Sometimes it's a gadget, but sometimes it's a method, taking something direct but unpleasant and turning into something complex but appealing (and something that usually doesn't work). But often our question is just a mask for our statement: I don't want things to be the way they are but I don't want to do anything to change them. If we only accept what is, buckle down and face it, it becomes less of a problem that skirting the problem, feeling stress, searching for answers not there, fighting an unresponsive reality.

Q. Grower: How do I deal with having a dog and raising flowers?
A. Get rid of the dog or train him.
Q. How do I find time to go on vacation?
A. Don't go on vacation or quit farming, or go on vacation and let the business suffer the consequences.

Q. Grower: How do I deal with having young children on the farm?
A. Well, you can't really get rid of the kids, so train them or get someone to help.

These answers sound heartless, perhaps, but who's more heartless, the person who wants all of reality to change or the person who tells her the truth about reality? We all want easy answers to unsolvable questions. That's how we're born, helpless, wanting everything and able to do almost nothing, and the longer our families and teachers enabled our weakness by doing our tasks and answering our problems instead of letting us deal with consequences and figuring out by ourselves how to deal with things, the harder it will be to overcome our training. I remember starting to farm, how I wanted my hand held—heck, when I'm confronted by something new, I still want someone to take care of the unknown or the mess I made, but now I recognize the symptoms of regressing to toddlerhood, that tightening up, scrunching up my face in a pout, my internal voice turning into a whine, and in an instant I know I'm just making things worse—and I deal with it myself.

Being a farmer brings us into the adult world where we live with the problems we make or change the situation we're in by changing ourselves. It's a step into freedom from tantrum-throwing, from expecting either magic from the world or wanting Mom to save the moment.

Tip #23. Quit tugging on mama's skirt. All of us start into the world asking questions, usually to our mothers. If we had good parents, they taught us to start figuring out things on our own so that our lives didn't overwhelm theirs. It's called "learning to learn"—we learn to not touch the hot stove, then learn not to touch all hot things; we learn to not touch the sharp knife, then learn to not touch all sharp things. If someone has to answer all the problems and questions in your life, they have no life of their own!

Google's become everyone's Mama, I'm afraid, and the more you rely on it the less adult you are and the more you depend on others—and the less you actually learn. Thinking comes from grouping facts together, linking them into tendencies and ideas, and Google can't do that for you. It's okay to ask where to get seeds once, but once you understand where the "gettin' place" is (my favorite line from the movie "All the Pretty Horses"), check for yourself to see if it offers the other seeds you want instead of asking someone else first. Same for plugs—if someone tells you where to get plugs for a species by giving you a list of suppliers, use that list to find other species you want, rather than asking every time, imposing on others rather than doing the work yourself.

Do your homework. The world is filled with teachers and helpers, but even the best and most saintly tire of those who want not help but someone to do things for them. Show up at the IRS audit with a boxful of receipts—see where that gets you. Tell the cop to find your registration in your jockey box—that'll work. Ask a question that's already been answered, ask for directions already stated in what you've been reading, expect the whole class, who've done their homework, to wait while the teacher explains to you, who hasn't, what the homework was meant to give you—you get the message.

Many times I've seen posts on the Internet from people who've done nothing more than purchase land but now want others to tell them how to start a flower farm, how to grow flowers, how to sell flowers—and they've not even read a book, they haven't done their homework, they haven't *learned to learn*. If you need a proverbial injunction to express what I'm trying to convey, here it is: give a man a fish and feed him once, teach him to fish and feed him for a lifetime. Ask away, but do a little of your own investigative work first. Just as Slow Flowers is about paying attention to the entire farming process rather than giving in to easy buying impulses, asking questions is about trying to answer them by yourself first, working your mind, discovering connections, and only after failing asking for help.

PART THREE

THE DEADHEAD EMPLOYEE/ EMPLOYER HANDBOOK

IT'S ALL ABOUT YOU

I T'S ALL ABOUT you.
To you, that is.

And it's all about me. To me.

It's about him to him and about her to her. Six billion times over. Which explains why things sometimes move fitfully—or not at all. It's a wonder order exists, really, given the constant battle between individual interests. It's especially surprising when our work with others goes smoothly.

I've looked at work from both sides now—wait, that's Joni Mitchell, singing about love, not work. But the song still holds true: give and take, up and down, and I still don't really understand work at all. But I'll give you what I've got.

If you employ people you'll nod knowingly at my confusion—unless you qualify for sainthood—because you know qualified workers are difficult to find. People who know how to work. People *willing* to work. People who put forth effort. People who can learn. People who can follow orders, who don't have to be babysat, who can work with others.

But if you're an employee, you're nodding, too, because your boss doesn't communicate well, doesn't do things right, doesn't really know what he's doing, doesn't give decent feedback, and so forth.

The other guy's always wrong, no doubt about it.

I worked on a commercial farm for fifteen years, off and on, and since my employer was my brother-in-law I tagged along with him during slack times—when it rained, when it froze, when equipment broke down, when things slowed down. We went to the local café where farmers and agriculture-related businessmen regularly gathered for coffee, and there I listened to bellyaching about workers and their shortcomings. It goes without saying, I suspect, that I frequently thought "bullshit!" but never said it.

My version of the story went something like this: the bosses sit on their asses drinking coffee while those *worthless* workers take care of their farms, moving pipe, driving tractors, picking rock, hauling commodities, spraying chemical from dawn to dusk.

Resentment, you might correctly decipher, fuelled my days.

Now, as a cut flower farmer who employs just a few part-time workers from spring to fall, I feel pretty sheepish, a little guilty and embarrassed about that attitude. I'm pretty sure I owe my old boss a series of lengthy apologies.

Not a day goes by on the farm that I don't recall the anger of performing menial tasks—and a heartbeat later wonder why I enjoy doing them now. It's a conundrum. A paradox. Certainly an occasion for irony. And I imagine sitting at the Chuck Wagon with my boss as a conspiratorial cohort rather than as an employee, commenting on the contradiction of experiencing both sides of the worker-employer relationship, fishing for a forgiving laugh as I offer up my unsaid apology.

There are some inherent properties of the employer-employee relationship that just can't be wished away or denied, and which despite the efforts of imaginative philosophers remain problematic. You just can't get away from authority issues, for instance—someone has to be in charge or the entire operation turns into a Tower of Babel and falls apart. But you can smooth over most difficulties by streamlining the relationship, simplifying it to its basics by identifying what it is and eliminating the baggage most of us hang on it. This part of *All Petal, No Pollen* aims to guide employees away from resentment, embarrassment, and self-recrimination, among other things, while steering employers from contempt, disdain, and surrender, hoping those who read it understand the complicated nature of the simple things they ask. Hopefully, it inspires a little empathy from each side toward the other.

PROBLEM WITH AUTHORITY

FIRST, THE DISCLOSURE: I lack any qualification to advise you about the boss-worker relationship since I've never held a real job. That is, year-round nine-to-five or anything similar to it. I worked at a factory for food processing for six weeks before finding out I couldn't handle shift work, inside labor, the drone of endless repetitive tasks, and working while my friends partied. I worked for farmers for short stints during planting and harvest, before I found out I couldn't tolerate the yoke on my time. I did manage to work one parcel of time when I was twenty-two that extended from February to November with only two days off of work, a testament to my stubbornness and my brother-in-law's patience. On and off for fifteen more years I worked for him, sandwiching in college semesters during periods when my distaste for work reached critical stage. That's the extent of my employed experience. But I have spent a lot of time thinking about work, if that counts.

When people asked what I did, I sardonically replied that I was "self-unemployed" but it wasn't a joke. It wasn't that I didn't want to work, or even that I didn't like to work, but I didn't know how to get a job and there weren't that many to get, and when I did get one I couldn't stand it because I inevitably felt chained to a dreary unpleasantness that extended not just for the workday but, in my mind, for eternity. I hadn't yet stumbled on Schopenhauer's admonition that any pain is bearable, that it only becomes unbearable when we imagine it as continuing on forever.

In fact, I loved helping people, loved the feeling of a joint enterprise, the nature of a task beginning, being undertaken, then completed. But the minute I felt like a cog in a machine, that I was just a thing among things required in a process to generate an end result, I'd get the feeling a wild horse gets when the bit goes in his mouth and I'd quit without any reason and feel grateful for weeks, as if I'd come up from the deep after being near-drowned.

Being a hippie, I needed little to survive and I had a tiny income on the side from raising leafcutter bees to supplement my needs, so I knew how to make seasonal job money last through slack times. And even years later, when I acquired a family, I scrambled to earn my keep without working for someone else. I trapped gophers, sold alfalfa seed, continued to raise leafcutter bees, then started raising flowers.

I was unemployable in the context I lived in, with a difficult attitude in a difficult situation, believing myself too smart to do menial tasks but knowing I was too dumb to do specialized ones, too proud to do the former and to admit I couldn't do the latter. I resented being told what to do, resented my time being someone else's, resented working for low pay while owners got rich, resented long hours, resented wearisome and tedious tasks. I even resented being inept when I wasn't feeling ashamed for being so.

I was self-unemployed, self-unemployable.

As for my experience as an employer, well, it's pretty limited, too. I've run a cut flower farm for twenty years and hired twenty or thirty workers for shorter or longer periods of time, and run across an assortment of people that span a pretty wide spectrum that ranges into the interesting, the odd, the frightening—which, as I've learned in my discussions with other employers, seems pretty common.

So I'm uniquely unqualified to write about the subject. On the other hand, how many crazy psychiatrists have you known, how many unmarried marriage counselors, how many coaches who were never very good at the game? You don't have to have extensive experience to understand experience, you just have to pay extra attention to the experience you do have or adroitly witness the experiences of others. In fact, sometimes experience can cloud your judgment, since you can come to conclusions that hold true from one vantage point but are wholly wrong in a larger or newer context (that's my defense, anyway).

Just as we can't occupy the same space, we can't really take up the same time. When we're together, any given moment is yours or it's mine, and all we can do is take turns over a sequence of moments or hog time at the expense of the other. It's like that exercise during group discussion where only the person holding the rock gets to speak and the others must listen (not saying they will). Every human endeavor in some way has this aspect.

But here it is. I'm the boss. You're the employee. It's not about me, it's not about you, it's about the task at hand. If either of us makes it otherwise, we've made a mistake.

If you have a problem with authority, get over it. I'm not your boss outside the workplace, not the boss outside the hours of work, authority here is phase-specific or task-specific. Just as when the plumber comes to your home, he's the boss over that specific task and you just foul up the works if you act as if it were otherwise, I'm the authority about tasks here on the farm. It's not because I'm ME, or better than you in any way, it's just that it simplifies things to have me in charge since I'm the one who bears the biggest brunt of any mistake. Likewise, just as your first grade teacher was the authority in the classroom and not your boss at church or at the bar later in your life, I'm above you in power only here, on the job. How else would anything work without some sort of hierarchy? Distasteful as it might be, I think an honest appraisal of the other choice, anarchy, gives it a better flavor. If you've ever been a part of a decision making process that was entirely democratic, I'm guessing you'll agree—it's amazing how many people just like to hear themselves talk.

Conversation-wise, if we're both talking no one's listening, and if we're both listening, no one's talking. There are only a couple ways out of this: one of us gets it all and the other nothing or else we share, and if we share, there's a long spectrum of possibilities that ranges from near nothing to almost everything, and we're always negotiating just where on that spectrum we wish to operate.

Somewhere on that spectrum I'm the boss and you're the worker.

There's a lot said about equality and in a perfect world we'd share just the right amount and be glad about it, but we all come in different types. Some of us are pleased with less, some of us are displeased with less than most, if not *all*, and some of us gladly let others take a bigger portion of the here and now, gathering our satisfactions internally, where space does in fact seem to come in bigger portions. Rarely, though, do we encounter a person who perfectly matches us to make a well functioning whole, that neither crowds us from our own expression nor leaves the space too open for our liking.

So a moment's about me and the next is about you, but sometimes it's about a third thing. If it's art or music, it's about that, and as you and I look or listen, we let that thing have it's due. And if it's a job, it's about the task to be done, not about you, not about me, but the task.

As an employee, I need to remember that. And as an employer, I need to remember that, too. *DON"T MAKE IT PERSONAL.*

Sometimes you're not helping when you're helping.

If a task takes two people, it may be twice as difficult, but its difficulty may rise even more dramatically than that. A third thing happens—my work, your work, plus OUR work, the interaction. But if someone takes the lead and someone follows, and the follower keeps following and the leader keeps leading, it's just one thing instead of three, a process easily remembered. The follower isn't less important or significant than the leader, except in the undertaking of the task at hand.

If you're the follower and it's a simple task you might have time to think about making it about you. You want to do a good job and someone told you that you should keep busy at all times, so when you're standing there waiting for me maybe you're feeling worthless, or maybe you want to score some brownie points, so you decide to pull a few nearby weeds as you wait.

Don't.

Theoretically, it would be a good thing to do, but in reality you're losing focus on the task we're sharing, and so I end up waiting for you to pull that weed and the process is slowed. It's about the task, not about me, not about you. Don't feel bad about standing around doing nothing, because that's exactly what you're supposed to be doing.

Just like a fireman is paid to wait around for fire and being ready to fight one when one occurs, you're paid to help me complete the task in as quick a manner as possible, and that entails picking your nose as you wait for me.

That's not the only variation of shared tasks, however. There's the one where we do the same thing in tandem, like rolling up tarps or lifting netting from one bed to another. This can be really confusing.

If a person on one end of a roll rolls faster than the one on the other, the roll will go wonky, so there's a constant flow of feedback between the two rollers, each watching the other to see if they're getting ahead or behind and adjusting their speed as they register the information. Theoretically.

What can happen, however, is one or both rollers tries to be alpha roller, and so adjusts his or her speed to the other's, but doesn't take into account the other's adjustments to him. This is difficult to explain, but let's try.

You're walking down the street, you run into me coming toward you on the same path. If you go left and I go right to avoid colliding, we run into each other despite trying not to, and if I go left and you go right, the same happens. Likely you've experienced this. Luckily the almost-clashing usually stops after three or four repetitions, but theoretically it could go on forever.

We've devised ways around these impasses. One is violence, which I don't recommend. Another is dialogue. Mostly we just solve it unconsciously with logic—instead of viewing the encounter as me against you, we have an out-of-occasion experience and view it as a whole and quickly see that one of us must go one way, the other person, the other.

Every human relationship is a clash on the sidewalk. Generally we only stay in relationships with those who negotiate that clash well—instead of bumping into each other constantly we, well, dance (without stepping on each other's toes, of course), anticipating each other's moves and sharing the moment. The employer-employee relationship is no different. It's two people heading right for each other on the same exact path, and hopefully at least one of them sees the other coming.

You may think I'm exaggerating but let's face it, employer-employee is just master-slave all over again, if a watered down version. However, the differences are stark—the time frame of my authority lasts only so long, if I make it all about me you can quit, and if you make it all about you I can fire you. Everything else is negotiable, including the way we behave toward each other. We can keep running into each other or we can dance.

But it's still not about you, and it's still not about me, and while it is about you-and-me, I'm the reluctant lead. As an employer, I don't want a relationship, and as an employee, you probably don't either, even though we've watched those Hallmark films of a boss mentoring a greenhorn, taming him or her and making a full fledged realized being from unformed clay. Yeah, I cry, too. We don't want a relationship, but we're in one—it's probably like an arranged marriage except the arrangement is made on the fly.

It can be unpleasant being an employee, though it

doesn't have to be. It can be just as unpleasant as an employer. Having been the former, let me assure you, the latter has only one thing going for it: power. As an employer, I can take fifteen minutes for a break whenever I want to or refuse to do something I don't feel like doing. I'll pay for any bad behavior, it's true, but I do have that choice that the employee doesn't.

But all the other little annoying things in the relationship are as bad if not worse for the employer. The main reason I became one—other than the fact I was unemployable—was to quit being an employee, so I assure you, now that I know it's just as bad on the other side, I only hire you as a last resort, not because I want to but because I need to.

So don't expect me to be nice. I should be nice, it's true, just out of general principle, but I may have other things on my mind. Like where a load of flowers is going, what needs to be cut, the aphid outbreak on the snaps, the roadways needing sprayed, the new transplants needing irrigation, the ground needing to be tilled for next week's seeding—among other things. I hire you to lighten my load. If I have to be nice, if I have to chat, if I have to pat you on the back every time you do something well, you're not lightening my load. Instead of dancing, we're running into each other.

I know, I know, when I was your age I had read Marxists, too, and I resented my employer when he didn't conform to my idea of an ideal relationship, but I didn't have a job description like this one I'm giving you, the one that reads: it's not about you, it's about the task. I may be just as sorry as you that we can't be friends, but I can either continue to have a business that works or I can be your friend during work hours and let the business go to hell.

It's about the task. To the extent either of us makes it otherwise we're acting mistakenly. There are a lot of ways to do that, and we're likely to partake of many, if not all, of them.

RESPECTING WORK

I CAN'T HELP YOU if you're looking to enter the corporate world or a bureaucracy, since the thought of that act intimidates me as much as it might you. My attempts to join the "official" work force proved pretty pathetic (I seem to recall a lot of sweating and my left eye twitching uncontrollably), and though I think I could probably give a better go at it now than I did back then, the idea of trying still makes me queasy.

It's funny, if you think about it—why should asking for a job be intimidating? But there it is, a wall—an imaginary one, but nonetheless there it is—you have to break through, there's an *inside* that you're *outside* of, there's a way to act, a way to dress, a secret code entailing right speech, right gesture, perhaps even a handshake or password you have to know to enter. It's like those fairy tales you learned as a child, where the peasant has to answer a riddle to save his life or family, a riddle that he has no idea as to its meaning. It seemed so, to me, and even forty years later and after numerous sociology and philosophy classes in college and a few forays into the real world, even after I know those imaginary things are just phantoms I also know that the world takes them as real.

But if you're entering the work force at a low level job like the one I'm offering, you won't have quite the intimidation factor of applying for a job at Bechtel with its forms and receptionists and interviews and antiseptic rooms. After all, there I am in my muddy boots, torn shirt, grizzled face, greasy hat, hardly an intimidating factor. But you may find the same walls that seem difficult to surmount, and having been on both sides of the wall I'm going to give you the best advice I can to climb right over or bust right through it.

You have to remember a wall has two sides, that it's a border that connects as well as separates. As an employer I may be inside and you outside, but at the same time I'm outside the world you're inside of. In a sense we're even. But even though we're on different sides of the wall, we're connected AT the wall, we're in the same time and place— let's call it an occasion. We're employee-employer—not employee or employer—one occasion, not two. You're coming to me in need, but I'm going to you in need, too. It's not an antagonistic relationship, it's cooperative and complementary.

Climb inside. Now that you're here with me, stay. That means you have to quit looking at yourself. What do I mean by that, you ask—well, quit perceiving yourself as an object, quit being on both sides, being self-conscious, judging yourself as inadequate or on the other hand as overqualified. You're making this difficult, and it's simple, because you're trying to be in two places at one time. You're trying to be inside the occasion and outside looking in, you're trying to act and you're watching yourself act, and no one's been able to do that on a regular basis yet, though mystics and charlatans alike keep trying.

One of the ways of being outside the occasion (and simultaneously, inside) that a lot of entry level workers use, and I count myself as having been one of them and if I weren't an employer I'd be one again, is to have too much pride to ask for help. We feel like asking for a job is a bit like begging. An anthropologist wrote a great book called *Talley's Corner* that tells about a group of unemployed men who gathered on a city street corner every morning where employers drove by to find temporary workers. A lot of the men, though needing work, refused minimally paying tasks because they were so down and out they valued their pride over a few dollars made from a crappy job. It's an unfortunate emotional stance I understand all too well.

Let's face it, there's a submissive-dominant aspect to the whole work relationship, it's a power thing that inspires resentment. But it doesn't need to.

So you're going to have to give it up. Pride, I mean. And the whole problem with power and authority. I *am* asking you to do my bidding, it's true, but I'm a slave, too, to the job, it just happens that I'm on the other side of that wall, in charge, trying to streamline a task. Hopefully, doing so benefits you as much as it does me.

If pride's not your problem, you may instead have a problem with respect—lack of respect for the guy who works a lousy job. For all the lip service given to Americans for appreciating hard work I give a big Bronx cheer, because there's not a soul I know that wants their daughter marrying the janitor at the school rather than a stock broker or someone else who doesn't get their hands dirty, the less hours of work they do, the better.

Americans I know (and I live in one of those put-work-on-a-pedestal red states) don't really respect work. How do I know? Well, I frequently get asked what we do and how we do it, and when I detail the manual labor involved in planting twenty-five thousand tulips or ten thousand seedlings, they not only express astonishment but look at me like I'm just a bit crazy or stupid, perplexed that we don't buy a machine to do it for us—*when they don't even know if such a machine exists!* It's that old reliance on magic or technology, anything requiring exertion is a problem that can be solved with a machine or a method.

People don't respect work, let's face it, and you probably don't, either. You've probably made fun of the guy at the MacDonald' counter, or the busboy, or the janitor, so it's no wonder you can't imagine yourself with a hoe or a shovel. Once you play the role of the critic you tend to criticize not only others but yourself—call it the mirror effect or the boomerang syndrome, but you can't hardly help from being ashamed when you have to take a job like the one I'm offering, because you've been shaming others for doing the same thing or the equivalent.

So next time you find yourself making fun of someone

for doing a job, cut yourself off, slap yourself on the hand and move on to a better viewpoint, because that voice you're letting loose is boomeranging back toward you and preventing you from doing the work you need to do, from respecting that work, and then doing that work well and getting a great sense of accomplishment from it.

Pride can be a terrible thing. If you're too proud to ask for help, how do you expect to get it—do you think it just falls into your lap, a gift from the Gods? Everyone needs something, it's the nature of life itself, and if they don't need something they want it—just ask the Buddha, whose entire philosophy rests on the nature of desire as the root of all suffering.

Remember, the boss is needy, too, or he wouldn't be asking for help. He's got his hand out begging just as you do.

GOLDILOCKS

G OLDILOCKS. YOU KNOW the story. Too much, too little, just right. Too hot, too cold, just right. Too big, too small, just right. Remember the story and take it to heart, because if you incorporate it into your understanding it's worth at least twelve college credits. And on our farm, it's another four bucks an hour.

It's obvious, I know, but suffer through this for a moment. You can even roll your eyes, just humor me, because it's more complicated than it seems, or should I say it's just richer.

There's a subjective component to the Goldilocks story, but a second hidden component, as well, that resides outside it. First, the subjective. Each bed, each bowl of porridge, may be just fine for the particular user— mama's bed for mama, papa's bowl for papa, baby's chair for baby—but not necessarily for Goldilocks. That's the subjective part. It's contextual. "Good" and "just right" are judgments of the particular experiencer and not qualities on their own. It's like up and down—if I'm standing on my head and define my "up" as the direction from my eyes toward the top of my head, then my up's not your up. But as a species we define "up" as that direction away from the earth and toward the sky, making it a word and concept that we all share at any given time. Never mind that our "up" wouldn't be the same "up" to those on other planets—that's a different story, a bigger picture, a much bigger occasion.

It's also like left and right—if my left is to the east and you're facing me, then your left is to the west. If you're like me, you wondered at one time why up and down weren't reversed in a mirror like left and right and here's your answer: east and west (objective notions) aren't reversed at all, only left and right (subjective concepts) are.

Each perspective has a different viewpoint regarding what's "good" or "right", and you'll find that's true here on the farm, where my perspective is "right" only because I pay the bills. It is, in this sense, all about me. What's more, my "right" may differ from day to day, whether it be due to a change in customer demand or a momentary alteration in my character from drinking too much coffee. Roll with it, I'm not judging you as being wrong. I may say that *this* is the right way to do something, but what I really mean is it's the way we do things *here at this moment.* Treat it as a fact for the moment, but one that might be discarded if you move on to another time and place.

But there's an underlying objective theme, too, to the

Goldilocks story, if you consider the too big-too little-just right and its companions as illustrations of a spectrum, a continuum that most things in nature exhibit. Just about everything in the world appears in a spectral range, with liquids changing to solids or gases as temperatures change, materials hardening or softening, individuals within a species varying in size, shape and color while retaining a genetic likeness that allows them to interbreed. Light is comprised of a spectrum of colors as displayed by a rainbow, and if you're a flower farmer you kind of need to know the differences along that spectrum.

If you're religious, you likely learned about the world in blacks and whites, bads and goods, sinners and saints, that sort of thing. And if you've gone to school, you've learned from an early age the opposites—cold, hot; big, little; tall, short; etc... While some of your teachers may have actually believed there were only two categories of things, for most of them it was just easier to teach you that way, because two categories are simpler to remember than two hundred or two thousand. They figured someone else would fill in the blanks later—though they'd be wrong, unfortunately, in a great number of cases.

Now you're going to have to unlearn all that, but it shouldn't be any harder than finding out that Santa Claus isn't real—sorry to spill the beans for those of you who still believe, but maybe it's time to move on.

We can still think of opposites, but just as the employer and employee are two parts of one occasion, all the opposites are connected to each other, too. If you're acquainted with Taoist thought, you already know about this, and if you haven't read the Tao Te Ching and you want to be associated with nature you probably ought to take a look at it, because Taoism is a nature religion and it'll teach you a general way to look at things that serves you well in the field. You certainly don't need to pick up the belief system and customs that attend it as a religion, but you'd be amazed at the wisdom it offers for someone involved with living things.

The Taoists put their opposites in the Yin-Yang symbol, that circle with two fishes hugging each other, one black with a white eye, one white with a black eye, to symbolize the unity and balance of opposites. For them the opposites comprised one thing, a whole balanced by opposing but equal forces, and the proper way of living exhibited that balance in all ways.

The Greeks did something similar, placing opposites on the end of a spectrum. Perfect virtue, for instance, falls smack dab in the middle, not on the ends. Bravery fell not on the end but between fraidy-cat to stupid risk taker, and you weren't either spendthrift or miser but generous, right in the middle.

Most of life lends itself to the spectrum model, and you'll want to adapt it to any workplace you enter—or for that matter, any relationship of any kind with other people or any thing. Every virtue can be a vice—the tenacious person easily turns into a stubborn one, and the fastidious individual may transform into obsessive-compulsive. Cleanliness may be next to godliness, but it may be easier to live in a slob's house than in an overly clean one, where the inhabitants must worry more about the mess they might be making than getting on with a normal living.

Any workplace, like any home, likely has its own standards. We're at A- here for most things, because we think a little effort goes a long way toward achieving maximum output and the extra effort of perfection shrinks efficiency by requiring more exertion for little gain. If you think about it a little, you may realize that the urge for perfection may be the culprit in the supposedly deteriorating world—a few good rules result in ordering the world while extra ones that refine the problem just exacerbate it. Aim for the middle. You know, *just right.*

THE INTERVIEW

———···❦~❧❦···———

MEETING SOMEONE NEW is always a challenge. Meeting with a potential employer, that's even moreso.

There's an art to presenting yourself—it's called acting—and while those best at it might claim they're not acting at all (and who knows, maybe they're right) more likely they've just had more practice and have unconsciously assimilated enough feedback that they can make a good impression with ease.

For the rest of us, it's a trial. You have to think about what the other person wants, how you are, what you should say, what their responses mean, who you are exactly, and the list goes on. "Be yourself" is a common bit of advice, but what exactly is "yourself"? Is it that goofy guy that likes to joke around or the serious one, the snarky one or the deferent one?

In a fit of wanting to belong to the normal work

world, I had a few interviews so know how difficult they can be. I once applied for a government security job and was asked if I belonged to a communist organization, and I unwisely joked that I'd been called "a commie pinko fag" before. My reference was to a friend who often joked with me, but the joke fell flat on the interviewer and I spent the next twenty minutes trying to extricate myself from my faux paus. I'd just as well got up and left.

I also wore a borrowed suit to the interview, which no doubt the interviewer could tell from its ill-fitting nature. And midway through the interview my eye started twitching and never stopped for the next half hour, a result of a bit of advice to "make sure I made eye contact."

Any interview's probably going to end badly, but you'll learn from any interview. Go in thinking of it as an exercise not for this job but for a future one, take the pressure off. And don't beat yourself up over it and quit trying, because here's the thing: there are only four possibilities on a truth table here, you can succeed and get the job or fail, and you can try or not try. If you don't try, you surely fail, but if you do you might fail but you might succeed. Your only possibility of succeeding is trying.

CLASH OF OCCASIONS

THOUGH BOTH YOU and the boss are needy, it's still the boss who has the power, it's true. Not all the power, since you can quit, but he defines the task, defines its parameters, defines the way it's done. You may think the task dumb, its parameters too wide or too narrow, and think you know a better way to do it, but the boss is—well, the boss. Your way may be better, the task may indeed be inane, and it might be smarter to narrow or widen the nature of the task, but he's signing checks and he gets his way. Check your ego at the time clock. It's not about you. Hopefully he checks his there, too, but since he's the boss he may very well not. After all, he's probably not as enlightened as you. Just older, richer, luckier or more powerful. In any case, in a better position to be the boss than you are. Get over it.

While we're on the complaining theme, here's another thing to think about next time you grouse about something on the job. Maybe you're not a boss, don't have your own business, aren't the manager, because you really don't want to be. That is, you may think you want to be, but you really don't want to be responsible. It's much more comfortable and easy to sit in the back seat and tell the driver how to drive than to actually do the driving. One of the most important things I ever learned was when I sat on a Farmer's Market Board of Directors and had to deal with a number of constant gripers in the organization. A fellow board member, wiser than me, told me that the way to deal with such individuals was to give them power, so we voted the worst complainers to be members of the Board and voila, they quit griping. And they weren't very good at being in authority, either. Suddenly, they were quiet, and not too long after they got on the board they got right off.

The same goes for employers—when was the last time YOU spent ten hours a day doing repetitive work, unable to rest when you wanted to, having no say as to how things are done, being constantly told what to do?

Put yourself in the boss's position, and if you're a boss, put yourself in the employee's position. Think twice, or three times, before you speak or act.

Any human interaction is an awkward encounter on a sidewalk. We devise ways to avoid such clashes—that's what rules and regulations are for, that's what social norms are for, to simplify matters so we don't have to act like animals and sniff each other out every morning to discover whether we're enemy or foe. And in the employer-employee relationship, there are easy ways and hard ways to go about it.

The simplest relationship has just one way to be, and the authoritarian one happens to qualify as simple: I tell you to do something, you do it. It's the simplest mathematical representation of being, yes or no, one or zero, and you can imagine it in almost any action. "No tolerance" programs, for instance, simplify an authority's task—either you do or you don't, and if you don't you're punished accordingly. If you're a parent, you understand this—if you've instituted a midnight curfew and your teenager comes home at 12:01, he suffers the consequence, whereas if you waffle about him being just one minute late or if you accept excuses, suddenly you're faced with a number of possible scenarios that can proliferate exponentially. Next time he's two minutes late. Then three. If you keep it simple, at the level of occasion rather than at the meta-occasion discussing the occasion, confusion lessens; if you step outside the moment and begin questioning it as being fair, moral, or right—residing in the meta-occasion— suddenly the headaches multiply. That's why altering the employee-employer relationship to fit any other pattern other than the simplest complicates things. If I need to be your friend, or your teacher, or your confidant, or your role model, I face a situation I didn't ask for—all I wanted was someone to do a task. And if you have to be a listener, have to agree with me, be my sounding board, hear my troubles, when you just wanted a job so you could pay your bills—well, I've complicated matters for you.

Any extra information in a system potentially disrupts

and even destroys it. Too much broccoli in the garbage disposal, too many movies downloaded on your computer, too many bodies in the cemetery, overloads the design, and telling your boss about your interest in moss lawns or your date the weekend before threatens the integrity of the relationship. In a perfect world we'd all come to work, share our tribulations and joys, dance a jig, smile and hug, get things done without a hitch, but it's not perfect here. So you may think it inhuman that I don't care about what your life's like, but turn it around: do YOU care about my life? I didn't think so—I don't really recall you asking about how things were for me. You were making it all about you.

Monday mornings are big on the farm. It's a delivery day, and I frequently rise at four am or earlier to load the trucks, and just before seven Jeriann comes out to check the load and adjust its contents to what she feels might be appropriate for that day's clients. She leaves at seven sharp and has a schedule to keep to for the day, so she's ready to roll, focused on the day ahead.

Many employees, especially new ones, place socializing first on the farm's agenda, however. They're so excited about their weekend or their own life that they don't make the transition to a new occasion: work. They start making small talk the moment they appear in the shop or see one of the bosses, yammering on about things others might deem inane but which they find extraordinarily interesting, or at best, things we'd find interesting if only they expressed them at appropriate times. It's a mistake we all make, I'm sure—I believe I can recall every single time I said something that no one else was interested in, when I said something I shouldn't, when I butted into an ongoing event with my own non-helpful interjections, so if you recognize yourself here I feel your pain. It's embarrassing. But common. Just back away. You don't have to feel bad or stupid, because it's not that we don't like you, it's that we're busy, focused, and have no room for anything extraneous unless it has something to do with the job, the occasion, itself.

There'll be lots of such moments in any job, when you klutzily walk in on something being done and confuse things or even anger others. Just back away, realize it's not you but the clash of occasions you failed to isolate and assimilate.

FEEDBACK

———— ···❦···❧··· ————

I N A PERFECT world you'd be given all the information you needed to do a job and to do it well. You'd get practice to do it, oversight as you did it, evaluations afterward. And your boss would explain things exactly as you needed them explained, because of course you have a specific way you learn best and it's a different way than the way everyone else learns.

It's not a perfect world.

Coming straight from high school, I discovered just that on my first farm job when one morning I was given the keys to a ten wheel Kenworth with an eighteen speed transmission. I'd never driven anything besides a three or four speed manual. Downshifting required a procedure— which was explained to me—that omitted the use of a clutch and necessitated a "feel" for engine speed, but horrific sounds exploded from the transmission every time I tried to implement it—"grind me a pound" is the standard joke referring to a gear-jamming driver. Rather than grinding the gears and breaking every other tooth off the complicated machinery below me, I stopped the truck at every hill that required a lower gear on my ninety mile trip, started the truck back up from the lowest gear until I reached the highest one I could utilize. I never did learn the "double-clutch" method my boss, his son, and his daughter explained to me, but eventually I did learn how to match a slowing transmission with the clever use of the accelerator pedal to make gears mesh to downshift.

Likewise, my training for my first day on a potato sidedigger consisted of less than five minutes of instruction, leaving a crew of twenty at my mercy in the hopes I didn't destroy the process. "Go do this," "go do that," "go there", "stop and pick up some thingamajigs,"—directions often came in the most minimal packets, and in pre-cell phone days I was on my own. I sometimes compared myself to Lewis and Clark off in an unknown wilderness, deciphering clues from the environment to get to my destination.

My ignorance alarmed me. I thought I was pretty smart, after all. And my bosses' assumption that I could do the things I was supposed to without being shown how led me to believe that everyone else knew something I didn't. I was accustomed to getting instructions in school from a teacher or a book. I never really got over the disorientation, though I did learn the art of mentally shrugging off the panic.

If you work for me, it's pretty much the same. Yeah, I know, I should understand your position in ignorance having been there myself. Having been uncomfortable outfitted with a new task of which I knew nothing, I'm well aware that I should instruct you more adequately than I do—but if I have to show you how, I just as well do it myself. There are just too many tasks of too short a duration to explain them all. You have to learn, learn fast, make mistakes, understand why they're mistakes, learn from them, change your behavior. It's a sink or swim situation, and I'm relying on you being able to take minimal instructions and make maximum advantage of them.

Ask question if you have to, but don't ask questions just because you are in the habit of asking questions—that's a habit schoolboys learn when they either want the teacher's attention or have so much anxiety that they can't handle the least bit of uncertainty. I hired you because I trust you, so trust yourself. Unless you're completed bumfuzzled, you'll probably do just fine since this operation doesn't approach the difficulty of rocket science.

Take feedback. From the world, from the farm, from me, from your cohorts. That feedback means judge your work, not yourself. If I say something needs to be done differently, do it differently even though your way may be better or right. It's just the way we do things here, that's it. We're not grading on correctness, just on doing the task as I want it done.

This brings in the Goldilocks method for most things. So maybe I think you're doing things too fast. Or too slow. Being too meticulous. Not meticulous enough. Planting too close or too far apart. It's just like shooting a rifle—shoot high, shoot low, sight in between to find accuracy. Tomorrow I may change my mind and you may have to recalibrate, but don't get mad at me for changing my mind and I hopefully won't get mad at you. Remember, it's not right or wrong we're looking for so much as your total obeisance to my will (just kidding, I really just want you to conform to my standards at the moment, which may have changed arbitrarily for a reason that would take too long to explain to you).

If I ask you what you think, it's because I value your opinion. If you're afraid your answer will be wrong and hemhaw around or go through the decision making process you're of no use to me—I've been through the decision process so don't need it reiterated, just need a different perspective *WHICH IS WHY I ASKED IN THE FIRST PLACE.*

We give ourselves feedback all the time. Even in the midst of experience, we assess what's happening and alter our actions. When an employee and I lift a tiller into the truck and it fails to go in smoothly, I notice the camper shell opening is an inch or two too small and that the tiller needs to be tilted to fit in. He, on the other hand, sees the failure as lack of muscle and exerts himself to force the tiller in. The shell window breaks.

Doing more, intensifying effort, sometimes works, but more often doing something different is the appropriate response. Speaking louder and enunciating more clearly to those hard of hearing may help you be understood, doing the same to someone who speaks a different language likely does not.

Sometimes an employee, knowing I disapprove of his work, rather than altering his methods or actions just tries harder. This rarely works. Instead, the amplified effort results in amplified mistakes—different, not more intense actions answer the problem.

Faster, harder, sometimes is necessary, and sometimes slower and gentler works better. There's Goldilocks again. Take weeding for instance—most newbies don't weed very well at first since they're unacquainted with the species and the aspects of the task. Upon being corrected after their first miserably failed attempts, almost inevitably they go down the rows more slowly in order to better see each weed. Unfortunately, the best way to weed is quickly, because the more you stare the less you see. You have to move at a pace that your brain works but your mind doesn't, because all the preconceptions you bring to the job and all the distractions you brought to work will seep into the task and occlude its proper completion. Let your brain pick up differences, trust yourself.

Typically, the academic setting provides feedback for students, and not only specific feedback, but inadvertently the practice of accepting feedback—dialectic, if you will. The teacher responds to the student, the student responds to the teacher, and the student, repeating the process hundreds if not thousands of times, hopefully learns the habit of listening, assessing the incoming information and comparing it to his experience, then altering or refining action (or not), just as a basketball player fine-tunes passing, shooting, defending skills over time by assimilating the success of earlier actions and, if coached, the advice of others.

Here we have Goldilocks again. If an employee lacks practice at receiving feedback (negative feedback, in particular) he may spiral inward, think of himself rather than the action being addressed. After hiring several homeschooled people we've acquired a tentative prejudice, since none have been able to assimilate feedback. It's not their fault, they've had fewer authorities to provide feedback and fewer chances to assimilate it—there may be just the mother and siblings, rather than different teachers each year and scores of fellow students to measure oneself against.

We all want to be rewarded every time we do something well, but I assure you, it just expands my job description if I have to do an evaluation for every task. Remember, it's about the task, not about you. Or me. If you're doing a bad job, I should let you know. I don't have to get mad at you (well, maybe I do) but I do need to correct you, and so let me add to the unfairness: you don't get brownie points, but you do get demerits. How else am I going to get you to do the job properly? The job you did wrongly may be impossible to repair, but any like job in the future needs done differently, correctly, so my aim isn't to belittle you so much as it's aimed at the future tasks to take place.

Probably somebody told you—a parent, a teacher, a church leader—to go the extra mile. Well, yes and no. Yes, if you know the lay of the land, have been at the job long enough to understand the workplace nature, the boss's preferences, but otherwise no. Maybe you see the rebar laying in a not so neatly piled stack on the ground and know a better way to store it. You take time off the job you were told to do, cut up a pallet, fashion some braces, and stack the rebar a better way. You're impressed with yourself, and you anticipate a pat on the head.

Sorry, no biscuit. It is a better way, it's true, but you took time off your job, so I paid for something I didn't want. And you put it in a place I didn't want things stacked because something else will be going there— something you were unaware of.

So no, don't go the extra mile.

A friend of mine who lost a large farm to a cratering potato market got a job at a government facility, a job where evaluations take place yearly. When his came due he received a bad grade because he was "always trying to make things better" and his employers didn't want things done better. They wanted them done the way they were supposed to be done.

So the extra mile he always went on his farm didn't work as a method where many people worked—if he did shift work, how would the other crews know about any changes he made; if other, less able, employees got it into their heads to change things, how quickly would order turn to chaos? It's a common sport to make fun of bureaucracies and red tape and laws, but by having a rigid structure the rest of life may become easier to negotiate. You just have to make sure there aren't too many structures.

So the task is just the task, nothing more and nothing less, and anything you add to it makes it something else. Let the worth of the job done provide your reward. There's something to be said for the intrinsic worth in things. After all, don't you find it a little depressing to watch athletes doing a little victory dance after every small success when that's just their job?

PREJUDICE

A DMIT IT, GO ahead, you have a set of prejudices regarding potential employees. It's okay! We all do. No sentient animal survives without making quick generalizations about their environment and its other inhabitants, though those generalizations are without a doubt wrong at least part, if not most, of the time. We assess the situation, monitor our experience, and assimilate the data to make projections about the future: don't touch hot objects, don't drive through ramshackle neighborhoods, don't ask a blind banjo-player's family for help. The problem comes after the pre-judging—if you don't acknowledge your prejudices as tentative and quite probably flawed, you may take them as truth and discriminate against others needlessly.

Even those who've never employed someone have heard this prejudice: *people just don't know how to work these days.* If you read Greek texts from a couple millennia ago you'll see that the older generation's been talking about the younger one like this for a very long time, but this time around there are some extenuating circumstances. The older folks among us may have stood alongside our parents as they worked, cooked, and even played, and in that setting we learned lessons that slowly accrued as we experienced the world. Our parents may or may not have been intentionally teaching us, but teach us they did, but who among us now has a job that our kids can come to and learn with us? If I work at a nuclear facility does little Bobby get to come to work with me and see how to work with others, what not to do, how to improvise, discover the little unspoken things that make a workplace and workday move smoothly? If I take the kids to restaurants are they learning to cook at home, clean, how to juggle ingredients and amounts, the best way to do a thing, what makes some things efficient?

Not many young people get the opportunity to learn from their parents, and if they don't play team sports or music they likely don't learn to work with others. What they learn comes at school, from books, from the "meta" place, at the knowing level rather than the doing and thus lacking substance, likely.

So as an employer you're the mom and dad now, you have to teach. Sorry. You know that prejudice about kids not being willing or able to work? Well, it's true, but not necessarily because of their own faults—the problem's not inherent but fixable. Unfortunately you have to do the fixing.

As you sort through resumes you'll learn about your

prejudices. You may think the star athlete for a small college will be energetic, a team player, a real take charge person that works well with others and learns quickly. You may be wrong—we were.

You may think the vibrant young man who wants to come earlier than specified, who speaks deferentially, makes eye contact, has perfect manners, might be a good fit for the farm. You might be wrong—we were.

You may believe the young woman who loves flowers when she tells you she's done weddings, who has a bubbly personality, seems friendly and pleasant, but when you hire her you may be disappointed to find she knows practically nothing about flowers or growing them—we were.

You may be impressed by a young man's work, though you were a bit nonplussed by him wearing open sandals, then be disappointed when he calls after lunch to tell you he has personal problems and won't be returning to work—we were.

You may think an old man with broken teeth and poor social skills won't be worth a damn, but you might be desperate, hire him, and discover he has a PhD and works better than anyone else you've ever hired—we did!

Some people may be out of shape but still be able to work well. Some work quickly and peter out, others work slow and steady and last. Experience counts for something, but sometimes it gets in the way. Some will verify your prejudices as they take frequent cigarette breaks, as they carry a box of crackers in one hand and a hoe in the other, as they come to the shop every ten minutes for a drink rather than have a canteen by their work. You may find an applicant overeducated, undereducated, overweight, scrawny, and you may find disappointment more often than not but when you find someone who fits you'll be thrilled.

HELPING

———— ❧ ❧ ————

WHAT IS IT to help someone?
Well, for one thing help's not about you. It's about the other person or the task in which you're both embroiled.

When early on we rented land for our flower farm, the landlord was extremely helpful when it came to doing things for us—but only if those things were his idea. If I needed him to wait to cultivate so I could use the wheel hoe to get closer to the plants to limit weeding, he wouldn't. Instead, he "helped" us by cultivating the furrows between the rows where the flood irrigation ran, and in doing so threw clods that hardened to rock and hindered the wheel hoe to the extent it couldn't be used. His help was hindrance, resulting in more work, rather than less.

Think of two kinds of hostesses, the one who just offers you lunch because you're there and the one who invites you over a week ahead of time and then proceeds to have the perfect table setting, the perfect separation of courses, and has orchestrated topics of conversation. In the first instance, it's about the guest and about the guest-host; in the second, it may be more about the hostess. Help implies a certain sort of submissiveness, if you will, not to the other so much as to the occasion, to simply erasing one's own ego—just as you would when you let a child learn to walk. You can be there, in the background, to help, but you don't have to help so much that you hinder.

Your ideas may not be helpful. You may be trying to help, but you may just be adding confusion to the occasion. Example:

A new employee, on the first day of work, brought his infrared thermometer so I could measure ground temperature in different places, by doing so know when to irrigate. Now, I know how to irrigate plants—I've been doing it on my farm for twenty years and on others for another twenty. I still find it one of the more difficult judgment calls of farming, so no doubt there's room for improvement upon my skills, but magic—technology, to others—wouldn't, in this case, be of any use to me. It's true, I might learn to use it and do a better job of irrigating, but in a mature system change is difficult to incorporate.

Another, immersed in the task of pounding rebar in the ground to support raised beds in the greenhouse, suggested I buy the stakes which construction workers use when pouring cement. Wider in diameter with a head to pound a hammer on and a pointed end to more easily enter the earth, such stakes would be better—unfortunately, they cost about ten times as much as a piece of rebar and I'd be that much less profitable were I to use them.

You may know a better way. You may just THINK you know a better way. But you don't know the entirety of the occasion—profits, expenditures, pitfalls—and you are just disrupting the boss's sequence of actions. It doesn't matter if you're right—go ahead, keep thinking you are, just stay out of the way and keep your mouth shut—when you're entangling the plan at hand.

Sometimes, help is not help.

DIALECTIC

I'M GOING TO introduce a useful term: dialectic. The Greeks kind of used it, Hegel reinvented in, and Marx brought it into the vernacular, but we'll use it more broadly than they did. In academic terms, it's the process by which a thesis or statement gives rise to its opposite, an antithesis, and the conflict between the two results in progress, a synthesis—which becomes a new thesis or, since we're bandying about terms, new occasion. Sounds complicated, but let's invent how the modern day dog and rabbit evolved and you'll see how easy it really is.

Long ago there were slow dogs and slow rabbits. The slowest rabbits soon perished, leaving the fastest ones, so the population as a whole increased their running speed. The slow dogs then started dying off since they couldn't catch the faster rabbits, leaving the fastest dogs to reproduce. The fastest of the faster rabbits then survived and the slowest ones died, creating a dearth of rabbits slow enough for the slowest dogs to stay alive. The swifter dogs lived, etc. etc. etc.

That's dialectic.

Every relationship operates in this manner unless it's staid and stale. Many cultures through the years wanted things exactly that way, orderly and stale, and so created caste systems and English aristocracy to keep things the same to some degree. The job site works best for the employer if it remains staid, although a vibrant dialectic can increase productivity for the operation as a whole and be more pleasant for the participants. It's just unlikely that the dialectic tends that way—instead, because it can advance rapidly it tends to overwhelm the slow changes of the job requirements. That's when drama enters.

If you surround any thing with more things, the first thing gets lost, and it's the same way with the original occasion, the job, when employees start to bickering, talking about one another, referring to the boss, grousing about the work, among other things. There's lots of self-help out there to tell you how to make these surrounding details, the meta-verse if you will, work for you in a positive manner, but in reality the easiest way to keep a workplace or occasion "clean" and uncluttered is to keep it simple, understandable and clear.

Remember when you believed in Santa? Your parents spent a great deal of effort making an imaginary world coherent using the whole Christmas guise. Then, there came a time when you had to unlearn all that—you're two different people, really, the pre- and post-Santa. The same goes for any information on the job. I'll tell you many things when you start, but many of those things, once you've learned them, I'll overturn by telling you the exceptions to the rule, expanding the context you originally were taught in to include new things. We learn, and then learn more, essentially, by unlearning what we learned. It's a string of occasions.

Dialectic works when dealing with others, but also constantly operates internally. Any time you look back at your self or look in the mirror you oppose yourself. If I correct your work on the farm, you may respond dialectically to me, but it may be more effective for true change if you respond to yourself. Ask yourself what you did wrong, what you were thinking, and question your methods—but not too much (remember Goldilocks), because if you attend primarily to your own thoughts you're not attending to the outside world where I need you to act.

We call internal dialectic self-consciousness, and if it proceeds dialectically self-consciousness proves productive. But if I turn my attention toward my self simply to punish it, if I simply feel guilty, if I just chastise myself as stupid, it repeats itself without advancing, makes a groove and then a rut in thought as well as action, and becomes a self-reaffirming system that gathers strength but provides no transcendence. No synthesis.

If you want to fix yourself, don't—fix what you do, and you'll be fixed.

DEFAULT

W E OFTEN GIVE "tours" to friends and family since a flower farm seems unusual enough to serve as entertainment. Often a diligent observer will bring me a tool I've left in the equipment yard—a can of ether, a grease gun, possibly a wrench—thinking I've lost or misplaced it. Unfortunately, I leave those items for a reason—I often try to hook up a piece of equipment and discover I need a lubricant to get the PTO shaft on the tractor, so after several times having had to go back to the shop I now leave a can of ether (which works well as a rust breaker) near the rotovators. I leave a grease gun there for like reasons, as I'm more apt to grease the equipment when I attach it than I am by driving it to the shop (it also leaves the inevitable mess out in the field rather than near the processing area). A hammer resides in the yard sometimes, so I can beat a pin in, and a set of waterpump pliers remains at a broken valve that requires them to open or close. the "returners" bear many likenesses: they're gadget guys, real fixit men, and no doubt they've learned or been told that you always need to put your tools back.

If you work alone, you can put your tools anywhere you want to. For instance, I often leave the tractor out in the field in mid-task rather than return it to the shop as one properly should. Or I leave a drip tape connector by the greenhouse door because I know one will be needed, eventually. But if you work with others there needs to be a default mode, a place where everyone can expect to find a thing. It's not the right place or the best place, it's just THE place that allows all the users to never have to think about it, to guess where it might be, to decide, to waste time.

The reason you put tools back where you got them from isn't because there's a universally written rule that there's a best place to put them. There may be plenty of better places, more appropriate places, but because there is a specific place it's supposed to be it allows that everyone who uses a tool knows where it is, rather than imagining what the prior user was thinking when he ceased using it—whether he left it at a prior job, out of misguided generosity decided to put it in where others could easily find it (but in fact can't), or out of malice, perhaps, hid it from others. The new user, having a default place, can just go, without thinking, without hunting, to the place it has been agreed upon that the tool will be put, grab the tool and use it without thinking.

A lot said, there, for such a simple thing, but the default mode seems to be endangered everywhere nowadays, since everything's being questioned, so it needs to be unpacked from its tawdry coverings. Authority reeks of nastiness, and default mode is authority, even though it's sometimes just convenience. But just imagine what life would be like if everything had to be questioned, if we couldn't assume we'd already agreed on things being a certain way. Sure, the speed limit and highway laws may be unfair, but having them allows traffic to flow rather than proceeding in fits and starts (just take a gander at the traffic in countries where such laws aren't enforced). Maybe you think the monetary system's rigged, but without an agreed upon currency we'd be bartering with chickens and beads—just how far would your current lifestyle go with that? Banks open at a certain time, goods are sold in specific weights and numbers, we construct buildings along guidelines that, if enforced, allow buyers to trust they're getting something sturdy. If we didn't have defaults, we'd be like two cats that have to test each other out every morning, smelling, hissing, circling, until we've decided that, while we may not be friends, we're not enemies. Question, by all means, but don't take it to the level of annoyance.

So, in short, I'm not asking you to do what you're told because I want to boss you around, I just want to set the occasion to default so it moves more smoothly.

CONCLUSION

S O, MAYBE YOU'VE wasted your time reading this, we haven't told you anything that you don't already know. Employers, you already know that you ask too much and ask it in a way that seems intelligible and obvious to you but which is complete gobbledygook to the hiree. Employees, you already know that you pay more attention to your own daydreams than to the job, that you hate asking for a job, resent doing it, would rather be doing something else.

But maybe you learned something. You both need to know that it's not about you but about the job. Employees should know that there's a hierarchy not of who's better than who, who's smarter than who, or even who's richer or more powerful than who, but who is in charge and who isn't, and not for a reason of exploitation, snobbery, or evil but just because a hierarchy simplifies how things get done. There's one boss instead of two fighting or negotiating over every detail.

And maybe as an employer you can cut a little slack

and try remembering what it was like to work for someone else.

And maybe, just maybe, the single occasion of employee-employer turns to a pleasant dialectic that sends both parties on their way to sidewalk confrontations more easily bypassed.

Printed in the United States
By Bookmasters